Early Poetry

I0517714

Auguste de Villiers
de l'Isle-Adam

Translated by Richard Robinson

Sunny Lou Publishing Company
Portland, Oregon, USA
http://www.sunnyloupublishing.com

Corrected: 2024 August 4
Original Publication Date: 2024 August 3

ISBN: 978-1-955392-72-3

# # #

This translation from French is based on the
"Premières Poésies" section of *Villiers de l'Isle-Adam:
Œuvres complètes,* Tome 1, Éditions Gallimard, 1986.

The translation of the poem "Ballade" is based on
"Ballade" published by L. Tinterlin and Company, Printer;
Rue Neuve-Des-Bons-Enfants, 3, Paris; 1858.

Proofread by Alan Jue-Fan Robinson

Contents

Preface

The author of this volume is nineteen years old. – It is therefore with a certain modesty that he releases these first pages.

– *November 1858.*

Nocturnal Fantasies

Barcarolle

Cœlumque tueri jussit[1]

    – OVID

I

The stars are reflected in the blue waves of the gulf.
The wind that blows near the flowering lemon trees
Wafts to us, while making our white sails shuffle,
    The fishermen's barcarolles.

I love the distant songs of their fugitive voices!
They pass for a moment on the wind that escapes,
Impregnated by perfumes from the plaintive shore,
    Then... die in the night.

For night arrives, melancholic and somber,
With all its silence and all its beauty:
The sky is variegated with its innumerable gold
      flowers
    Whose light is bathed in the sea;

And the silver foam of solitary waves
Undulates to the ends of the immense horizon
And rocks our skiff, whose gentle curves
    Seem like those of a halcyon.

---

[1]*Cœlumque tueri jusssit:* Latin for "And he ordered the sky to be gazed upon."

Ineffable moment of ecstasy and harmony,
When the human soul hopes for immortality,
When love can give rise to genius
      In a dream of voluptuousness!

II

"Let's go!... sing, O poet!... before the years
That the past will seize and that God has given you
Have frozen your flight under their funereal coat;
Since your romances are born of sorrow,
      Since you can still sing!...

"But if you feel your heart weep beneath your smile,
Oh! would that the strings of your lyre broke,
And your song mixed with the sailors' songs!...
– Suffer alone!... – And, if your soul sighs very softly,
      Hand its plaint over to the waves' noise!..."

III

And for all that, we have in this life, brothers,
Ineffable moments filled with melancholy,
      When a man, consoled,
Contemplating the skies and their dark splendors,
Casts on them lovingly with moist eyes
      A look of exile!

Friends!... let us dream then, oh! in silence,
A half-drowned heart of love and hope!...
      – It lasts so briefly!
When reality lifts its veil...

Ah well!... the dream will go there, into a star...
    And we say, "*Adieu!*"

IV

Let's dream! The silver waves expand, solitary!
Their peaks shimmer at the end of the horizon...
And our skiff, rocked by the gentle waves,
    Floats away, like a halcyon.

– *Gulf of Genoa, March 185*.*

Arab Song

Just as the ardent Simoon
Blows furiously on the withered plain,
Fly!... and make your steel hooves shine,
        O my courser!
On a cloud of sparks,
My good black horse has wings!
His fiery eyes pass into the air
    Like lightning!

Amidst the numberless sultans,
In his somber dome-covered harem,
Tired of his wellbeing, the old emir
    Goes to sleep!
She waits for me, his young slave does!
– The scimitar that I brave
Watches in silence, and knows how to crawl
    The better to strike. –

Oh!... by Kaaba the Accursed!...
Let's go, my horse, run swifter!...
You will bathe your black breast
    Near the seraglio!...
Friend, the sand is hollow perhaps,
The night, obscure, and the darkness, treacherous!...
– But the djinns guard the loves
    Of the giaours!

Giddyup! We'll pass at dawn
By the sonorous minaret,
Defying its hideous dervishes,
    Just the two of us.
– Or, if the eunuch's khanjar
This evening strikes my neck,
Your soul, in Allah's paradise,
    Will join me yet!...

A Bottle of Spanish Wine

Friend, I see lots of things in it!

Go on, this flask lived! – A sylph with rose-tinted
    wings,
That formerly escaped from a sun beam,
Smiled to her lovers from her vermillion prison!
The liquor gaily sparkled! – The pale complexion
Of the cork, that jailer, was colored itself
By her light babbling! – It was a divine arm
That poured us joy when it poured us that wine!

Now that, uncorked by us, and completely drunk,
The bottle is lying on the table there,

The sylph, flying away like a gay butterfly,
Has returned on high, on the first sun beam,
In order to bring again, at next day's dawn,
New smiles to human misery!

Exile

Stanzas

I

That one – he said, – is the girl of the beaches,
Where the pale Ocean arches its savage flanks;
Where the night, the rocks, those heavy sea piles,
Ambush sailors, prey to the sky that groans;
Where, for ships at large wandering on the waves,
The wind digs a grave in their bitter wakes!

II

This one, whose face, ineffable prestige,
Bends in the evening breezes like a lily on the stem,
He's the child of lands where mangroves
Border the oases of faraway savannahs:
Where, in the shadows, one sees shining in the
          creepers,
The plovers' gilded wing like a vermillion prism!

III

The first one is a playful swimmer from Ischia
Who caresses the gulf with her alabaster arms
And smiles through her dripping hair,
While the tumultuous wave, whose foam unfurls,
Plays with her gorgeous body until, like a pearl,
Rolling it onto the sand, it dies at her white feet!

IV

The other one is a flower from those mild Antilles
Where, when moonlight silvers the arbors,
The frizzy mulatto extends his evening hammock,
And where the Southern night, with enervating
            delirium,
In a silent kiss that crosses their two smiles,
Seems to impregnate the temperate breezes with love!

V

Alas! in Paris, that lively furnace, when
I, exile's son, reflect on the cliff
Where a virgin voice joins the voices of the waves;
When I think of the forests where your soul dreams
Under long ebony trees, O creole with fiery eyes!...
– Ah! my solitary heart suffocates with sobs. –

VI

– O, my ancient loves, multi-colored Antilles,
And you, island rocks with purpled peaks,
You, I still love you, so why did I leave?

Among all these humans, lost, like an atom,
I came to search for glory, a vain phantom!...
Is it worth the peace that I yearn for today?

VII

Here devouring Boredom reigns supreme;
Here one does not hear the hymns at dawn;
Here one has lost the sacred delirium,
The holy enthusiasm that makes great things;
And smoke, from afar, has dried out the roses,
Roses that bloomed under azure skies!

VIII

Here the furnace rumbles, the factory ferments;
Molten energy boils in its burning lava,
For they want to join people together with them
In dismal unity; – hammers, on the anvil,
Fall again; on the rails, the steam engine whistles and
        fumes
To march toward an end that I do not believe in. –

IX

Here the peaceful gods of our fathers are laughed at!
Here are children who make their mothers weep.
Innocence has quit this place of fallen angels;
Immaculate lilies fall under the sickles.
Here all is withered in advance, O young girls!...
Here you are accursed... Here nobody loves any
        longer. –

X

Oh! when can I see that shore, where, formerly,
Silver fish scales in sunbeams
Scintillated on the sand... – and that vermillion land
Where the birds warble, – where the jungle tiger,
Under reddened bamboo, sleeps, retracting the nails
Of its lascivious paws, extended in the sun!

Indian Prayer

Foul is fair!

– SHAKESPEARE, *Macbeth*

On his knees, the brahman
Spoke, bowing his head
Before the black fetish:
"Grave witness of the world,
Brahma, help me sound
The oracles of evening.

"May my holy steps
Not encounter the footprint
Of Shiva, that fatal god;
Nor, before your silence,
The powerful alliance
Of good with evil;

"Nor on the savage rock,
The son of slavery,
The trembling pariah;
Nor on his impure hut,

Like a hideous augur,
The bloody Vampire.

"Nor the mournful joy
Of the Thug, ambushing his prey
To strangle him silently,
And then under the creepers
Like a djinn of the savannahs,
Hiding his accursed face;

"Nor in this wood that I enter,
Coiling its long belly
Up to the top of the palms,
The slick and green serpent,
Darting a fawn-colored tongue
Into the wood pigeons' nest."

Guitar[2]

Cadiz!

I

Now is the hour of serenades
When, far from the colonnades,
In the crystal flowing river,
    The silver star shines:
Spain, on these divine nights,
No longer hears the mandolins;
Many a beautiful eye will shut!
    – It's time for love.

---

[2]Guitar: This poem was apparently put to music by V. Loret in 1888. See note in *Œuvres Complètes*, Éditions Gallimard, 1986.

II

Girl, tomorrow you will
Dance your mad seguidilla
And put flowers, if you will,
      In your hair...
But, this evening, as the gypsy
Hangs his guitar on the plane tree,
Let's leave our golden hairnets there...
      – And love again!

III

The winds, passing o'er the waves,
With interlacing lovers' shadows
Blend the light foliage
      Of the orange trees...
If, near the monotonous river,
Orange trees and lovers
Must wither in autumn,
      – Let's love forever!

Chanson

FAUST: She leaves the church with a decent and contemplative air. Her eyes are moist. Look! She's an angel; she looks like she's exiting her house!

MEPHISTOPHELES: Today the somber altar, tomorrow the convent. And if you spoke to her quietly in the ear?

FAUST: What shall I tell her, given I love her?

MEPHISTOPHELES: Two words: I will whisper them to you!

– Faust, by the Author

Faust

Like a bluet that was placed
In the corolla of a beautiful lily,
    Oh! under your eyelids,
Your blue eyes shine timidly:
And they pure diamonds
    For an austere cloister!

Aren't you too young yet,
And the golden cup of loves
    Has it been drained?
Dry your tears with flowers, then,
Child, for they'll mistake your
    Tears for dew!

Zaïra

*"Whence comes it that you love in this way?" asked Sabid
again. – "Our women are beautiful, and our young men
chaste," responded the Arab of the Azra tribe.*

– EBN ABI HADGLAH, 1461-1462 manuscripts,
Royal Library

The setting sun, veiled, went down; –
A tepid air like a breath
Under the starred crepuscule
Floated softly on the plain. –

The Arab led his corsairs
Before the open tents.
– The plane trees and palm trees
Shook their long green leaves. –

A little farther away, his daughter,
All amorously inclined,
Was lying on her mat,
Her tanned chin in her hand.

Her black eyes, filled with languor,
Darkened her face with their eyelashes:
– Before her, the traveler
Stopped his wild horse;

And, leaning over suddenly, he said,
"Allah! how beautiful are you!
Do you wish to escape this accursed desert?
I love you and will be faithful to you." –

The child looked at him for a long while;
And, lifting herself up with effort,
"You are not the man I await,
O traveler with the ebony face!

"Another has already won my love;
And my love, it is my entire being.
I wait here for the giaour
Who will return, maybe this evening!

"But... this amber necklace, do you want it?
Take it! Here! and may Allah protect you!" –
The unknown man's gloomy hand

Fingered his dagger, undecided. –

"O, pearl of the desert! tell me:
And if the infidel giaour
Did not come back again?" –
"I understand your gist," she told him:

"But, my name is Zaïra.
Move on, – my heart loves him anyways:
I am from the tribe of Azra:
With us, one dies when one loves!"

Hermosa

A Poem

Song the First: Don Juan

I

The palace, that evening, shone under the arcades;
From the stairs to the balustrades
The white marble walls were bordered in purple.
Count Antonio spent his youth
Among the sounds of gold, love songs, drunken
　　　cries,
　　Clinking cups and dice!

II

The orchestra, gliding on the waves, in the gondolas,
Blended, bathed in the shadows, the voices of the
　　　barcarolles
With the charming splendor of its harmonious
　　　treasures.
Through stained glass windows open to fresh gusts
　　　of breeze,
One saw indecisive forms whirling,
　　The bouquets of women and flowers!

III

The hall sparkled with fires and finery;

Roses, like stars, decorated the heads of black hair;
Mirrors flamed with the marvels of the ball;
Voluptuousness closed their eyelids partially;
The interlaced couples waltzed, under the light
    Of gold and crystal lusters.

IV

A waltz has its pleasures, – above all in Italy,
The land of Raphael, where Melancholy
Promenades an ardent languor under the myrtles,
Where the virgin, it is said, a prey to vague fevers,
Opens for her young lover, while their lips unite,
    Her heart's perfumed case.

V

Love, it is the golden-faced aureole of these festivals.
The women of Venice have their silent dances,
They don't say much, – but their eyes are so
            agreeable!
But the coral folds of their divine smiles
Of enameled pearls seem also to say to you:
    "I know what you're feeling!"

VI

O Muse! one of these evenings, with youthful heart,
I want to bring my mistress to Italy!...
We will love, the two of us, the passing pleasures,
And we will join in the waltzes of Venice,
Under the domes of snowy flowers that the breeze
    Leaves on the orange-tree leaves.

VII

Or, perhaps, I will go there, – O intrepid barques! –
To find, one day, on the vague rapids,
A soldier's death worthy of my pride!
– Human race! Byron found you ungrateful...
For all that, he knew how to disembark in Roman
       sandals
   On freedom's shore.

VIII

Yes, I could die like that! – Not for glory...
What's the point? – Only, it would be nice to believe
That a child of Italy, with a gracious laugh,
When I have a black sheet over my face, a candle at
       my feet,
Might come and, smiling, place his rosary beads
   Beside the name of my ancestors!

IX

I would only do that insouciantly:
Laugh, sing, sleep; – it's boring, France!
And a man who is bored is capable of anything!
Then again, I don't like those who say: "What folly
It is to do a great deed at life's expense!
   Scornful oblivion lies waiting at the end!"

X

At the end of what, sirs? Do you estimate in essence
That it is not better to be purely human,

In other words, to love, to live, to die nobly,
Without wishing to get too involved in the things of
       this world,
Than to repeat forever that barren phrase?
    As for me, here's my sentiment:

XI

In his sacred pride, when a man succumbs,
What does the nothingness and oblivion of a tomb
       matter?
He knew how to live and die in his far-flung disdain:
What is it to him, – discourses murmured over his
       bier?
Grave, he rests there, draped in a shroud,
    Deaf to the vague cries of men.

XII

But he who only knows how to eat and drink,
Whose impotent disgust slavers over each glory,
Who buys a stupid kiss every night,
And who comes to deny God, glory, love, the soul's
       flowers!
In my eyes that person is nothing but a loathsome
       wretch,
    As much to be pitied as disdained.

XIII

If philosophy is meant to laugh at everything,
Goodbye Kant and Schelling! I prefer to see life
Or death, but from their finest angles;

And I admire a hero by pure materialism,
Without restraining the goal with too much cynicism,
    For it is fine to be a hero!

XIV

You are about to tell me, I know, that the aurora
Is nothing but a blue or pink *vapor*, that one is not
        ignorant
Of any of the *elements* with *um* in their name
That make up a *lily*; that love is not in vogue
Except in Mr. *Dorat*[3] or some other rhapsody;
    That it does quite well in an album;

XV

Et cætera... – Agreed. But, after all, the aurora
Is not less sublime, and the flowers it tinges with gold
Stay beautiful forever, with their charming scents!
The names in *um* are all very nice! – Me, I prefer...
– Good! The first bluet has appeared... (but without
    Too many naïveties). –

XVI

As for skeptical love... – O Stendhal! Has everyone
Had his say on the profound page,
Well formulated, well concluded, well disputed, my
        God?...
Me, having posed nothing, I wish to conclude
        nothing:
Only, my mistress is stunning, – and nature

---

[3]Dorat: Claude-Joseph Dorat, 18th-century French poet.

Has always a patch of blue sky.

XVII

Two years have passed already, I'm not the same.
– But it is essential finally to have a system,
Or everything becomes a deep chasm where our eyes
      grow dim...
In summary, – And our Hermosa? – What a bizarre
      prelude!...
Well, my cup of Cyprian wine, my cigar,
   – And let's continue our tale.

XVIII

I left you, I believe, at the ball of Count
Antonio at night, with the joyous swarm mounting
The palace stairs... – Behind the *cappa magna,*
The profiles of the madonna, glimpsed smiling,
Climbed like Giorgione's living ideals[4]
   Out of their enameled frames.

XIX

A thousand sprays of fire, from above the brown tiles,
Spangled the clear lagoon with their rubies;
– O Oriental golfs! – The masques, having escaped
The feast, ran off pell-mell; the almahs[5]
Held onto the perfumed gauzes of their satin scarfs

---

[4]Giorgione: Giorgio Barbarelli da Castelfranco, the 15th-century Venetian painter.

[5]almah: a sexually mature girl; potentially a virgin, but not necessarily.

With ungloved fingers.

XX

The hall sparkled with flowers and finery;
The roses like stars decorated the heads of black hair;
The mirrors flamed with the marvels of the ball;
Voluptuousness made the participants' eyes squint;
The interlaced couples waltzed under the light
    Of the gold and crystal lusters.

XXI

On a bronze plinth, at the back of the peristyle,
A woman was standing... unmoving.
At her feet the radiant beings twirled round.
Leaning her elbows on the casing, near the penumbra,
In a deep gaze she united, in the shadow,
    The fires of the ball with the night of the sky.

XXII

Oh! That woman was a sidereal beauty!
Her arms, models for Phidias or Praxiteles,
Supported her face with its marble traits;
The darkness decorated her spent pallor:
Thus lost in thought, she seemed
    The humans' nocturnal angel.

XXIII

Her thick, shiny hair under their black torsade
Framed the whiteness of her ivory temples;

Her face seemed to hide the creases of nights of love;
Chiseled in alabaster, shadowed in cornelian,
Her nose, straight, nuanced an aquiline curve,
    Like two lily leaves.

XXIV

Waves of black velvet were draped around her,
And the powerful flesh of her rebellious bosom
Roughly betrayed its shape when, with sighs,
It lifted her toga which was retained
On the nacreous curve of her naked shoulder
    By a small hook of sapphires.

XXV

She stood there like a phantom of Life:
In the whirling midst of ravishing entertainment
Her gaze was immersed, filled with dazzlement;
A star of diamonds, an ideal sign,
Consecrating her sovereign beauty, trembled
    In the reflections of her ebony hair.

XXVI

But one might have said that a dream enveloped her
With its splendid flight... At the caryatid's feet,
A din of pleasure fell like an affront:
One might have said that, fixing on her soul's
            innermost recesses,
The mute spirit of evenings, hovering above the
            woman,
    Batted its wings in her face.

XXVII

– Forget your terrible past, O enchanted statue!
Do you want existence? Just like Prometheus,
I can give it to you, with its despairs.
But you live as we do, for I see under the fringes
Of your long, jade eyelashes, those two strange tears
  Glazing the sparkle of your dark eyes.

XXVIII

Greetings, O you whom I love, O daughter of Spain,
O brigand's daughter! Laid to rest in his mountain
And in his freedom, your father is not alone:
His carbine is there, heavy, and of good calibre,
Keeping watch at his side! He was a free man:
  He sleeps in his loose shroud.

XXIX

We won't speak of him further. Forgetfulness, the
   second shroud
Of the solitary casket's livid captives,
For a long time now weighs on the bandit;
The brambles wind around his ruined cross.
What do the living care, who drink and sing,
  For those who have passed away into the night!

XXX

Ah! when under the pines shredded by the storm,
In the evening, he was king; in his wild sierra,
When he espied their steps, without respite, without

        rest,
And when on paths full of lugubrious traps
His familiar gunshot, resounding in the darkness,
        Bounded from echo to echo.

XXXI

He's remembered of course! Now? – O misery! –
If he'd been Caesar, that remainder of dust,
What good could it have served his accursed skull
To have worn, on the throne, a large diadem?
After all, everywhere, death is more or less the same,
        For the hero and the bandit.

XXXII

O, young people waltzing beneath this woman,
Be on your guard for her soul's abysses!
Waltz, waltz on! Don't look at her...
She is so far above this world, it seems,
She listens in profound ecstasy
        To the muted sound of the death carts.

XXXIII

In the past... – but how distant they are,
Those rapid years, from her forgetful heart! –
In the past, she was a child with pale traits
Who lived in the sun. She was the humble aegis
Of many travelers who implored her as a guide
        Across the gloomy coppices.

XXXIV

During the day she ran, a vision of Spain,
O'er the moss of the woods, through the green
   countryside,
And on the flank of mountains, far from the wander-
   ing flocks,
She sat alone, near old chasms,
And, a dreamer, she loved to cull the sublime flowers
  Growing near the torrents' edge.

XXXV

In the evening, she quit the plain and valley,
And returned for supper to the isolated hut...
He pressed her then against his beating heart,
And, near her, forgetting the mountain and storm,
His hand let fall on her cloudless face,
  Sometimes, a trace of blood.

XXXVI

Then, youth grew awakened in her soul,
– A rose so soon culled and so quickly without petals!
– She was ignorant, however, of the loves here below:
Her heart seemed frozen in her white breast...
– Then, one evening, she found herself orphaned,
  For the bandit never came home again.

XXXVII

So she went away, – sad mendicant child, –
Hiding under a cowl the bold curvature

Of her queenly figure with its splendid contours;
Serious, she went away to watch the young girls
        dance!
She heard the sound of silk and mantillas
    From a hiding place in the crossroads.

XXXVIII

But on the grass, in the glow of the blazing, setting
        sun,
She was never seen to share in their joy!
Only, when the happy young people waltzed,
When the Basque tambourine with its lively little
        silver bells
Accompanied the sound of the castanets,
    Her pensive eyes gazed on them.

XXXIX

One day, it seemed to her that she had arrived
In a deserted valley. The dawn, barely risen,
Lit up three paths before her exiled steps.
She was seventeen: – O phantoms of doubt!...
She saw that she needed to chose a route;
    She put her head into her hands. –

XL

"Young girl, you can choose; are you not beautiful?"
An immortal voice cried out to her from her heart. –
"Nothing troubles the azure of your triumphant sky.
My name is Virtue. Others, in silence,
Good for nothing, despise existence...

Come with me, my sweet child,

XLI

"Come, for I know how to enjoy work and the earth."
She heard these words, the austere young girl did,
But their real meaning for her was at that time
              obscure:
They did not satisfy her first distress.
And the child hesitated, envisioning for her youth
    A more abstract and pure desire.

XLII

Next to her suddenly, like a lily rising,
Another vision appeared in her dream;
Chaste, it pronounced these words: "I am Faith!
I am she who wears an expiatory mourning!
I am she who prays at the back of an oratory...
    My young sister, come with me.

XLIII

"The veil that God drapes over peaceful virgins,
Hiding the world and its visible loves from them,
Does not obscure their eyes to ideal love.
Come! Believe in suffering, child, it is a friend:
And the cloistered girl, asleep in her coffin,
    Rouses an angel in Heaven!"

XLIV

She did not understand. The sacred cellule,

Before her name, would have blocked her entry
            perhaps...
Could she not also live before dying?
She recalled the dances, the guitar,
The basques,[6] the joy and love that loses itself
      In the woods where the warm wind blows.

XLV

Hermosa fell silent, like someone who was asleep.
Another voice was already speaking into her ear,
Making ardent *tableaux* pass before her eyes:
Its words, fatal song, grim delirium,
Had, in their gaiety, a peal of laughter,
      Stifling a sound of sobs.

XLVI

"To live or die?" asked the voice; "but, old Earth,
What do you care? Aren't you vanity upon misery?
The freezing wind, that howls in the hollows of dark
            paths,
Carries lovers into the shadow where dreams go,
The leaves of the forest, the bitter waves of strands,
      And the changing waves of human beings!

XLVII

"Well! Let us also flee toward ever-closed nights!
Walking, let us cull all pleasures, those roses!
Let us go quickly, at the mercy of lenient laws,
Like those pure breezes that, o'er every plain,

---

[6]basques: a basque is a woman's tight-fitting bodice.

Bring sighs, kisses, exhalations,
   To the birds sleeping in the woods!

XLVIII

"Work, virtue, prayer! – for what? – One must live!
Leaf through, as a test, several pages of the book,
Smile... and close it without fear or regrets.
What of us remains? The humble shelter of an old
         tree;
Two words, quickly effaced, on a marble dome...
   And then oblivion, the king of cypresses!"

XLIX

She put her hands over her ardent heart,
Because a thousand passions battling in her soul
Then reflected a glimmer of hell there!
Just as one sees in the fog, prey to the wind of a
         storm,
The sinister finger of lightning projecting itself
         rapidly
   In the middle of a cloud.

L

When she lifted her immaculate head,
Evening was coming. The distant breeze, in the
         valley,
Dispersed the perfumes of the blossoming resedas;
One day had sufficed to change her face:
Death had already marked it with its cloud,
   Voluptuousness with its pallor!

LI

Now, all was finished. Beneath her eyelid
A tear trembled... but it was the last.
Disdainful, she had weighed Eternity:
Despair rejoiced with the somber locks
Of her fluttering hair and projected its shadows
    On the ideal of her beauty.

LII

Soon she heard a distant song:
A knight passing on the plain;
He seemed to be returning to the feudal manor
That stood beyond, there under the shining moon.
The knight mingled his insouciant voice
    With the sound of his horse's pace.

LIII

His name was Don Juan. He rode under the branches;
On his cap, haphazardly, white plumes flew;
His face seemed like that of a young man still;
He held the saddle firmly with his right hand;
His cloak, raised by his sword's handle,
    Exposed his golden spurs.

LIV

When he descried her, he said: "You're beautiful,
You who stand there!" – "Is that so?" she asked him.
Her innocence, weeping, vanished with those words.

"Are you from the sky?" – "Let's just say that I am! If
      it pleases you.
I love you!" – She smiled. He picked her up off the
      ground;
    Then they rode off at a gallop.

Song the Second: Existence

*He is the most handsome, poetic, and greatest person
anyone ever made!*

   – A. DE MUSSET, "Namouna"

I

From then on, it was forever for the two of them, a
      life
Full of elations, splendors, extravagances,
Dreams, feasts, dances, and commotion.
They were those who went to sleep at the crack of
      dawn,
And who, come evening, sacrificed again
    At the pale altars of the night.

II

They went along, without concern for the deep pit,
Exhausting at random the delights of this world,
The sources of joy and sensual pleasure.
Cadiz saw them sail away on an amorous wave,
Then Genoa the Superb, Palermo the Happy,
    And Naples with its enchanted gulf.

III

Ischia, whose banks are loved by poets,
Florence with its palaces, Parma with its violets,
Saw this couple pass with their carefree faces:
Like two swans that, far from saddening fogs,
Forever deploying their inconstant wings,
    Guide their flight towards other skies.

IV

But she soon saw inexpressible constraints
In this handsome knight with his quick embraces:
Don Juan, whom she had at first taken for a child,
At certain moments dropped his frivolous airs,
And frightened her almost with a word
    That he finished off with a smile.

V

O mystery! – She used to play near deep chasms. –
Ah well! When lost in intimate battles,
He fixed her with an eye glazed by obscure terrors,
She felt suddenly, while saying to him: "I love you!"
The same feeling of supreme vertigo
    That she had felt previously on the precipices of
        chasms.

VI

Yes! The mountain flanked by deserts, the stone cross
Of the accursed murderer,[7] the verdure and ivy

---

[7]murderer: viz. her father, the bandit.

Whose flowers crowned some devouring cave:
It was in that sense like a living mirage.
He seemed to her to hover over her savage destiny,
    Like an eagle over a torrent.

VII

Their life, this apart, was nothing but one long
        delirium.
Just as Hebe formerly, in her royal empire,
Poured the liquor of sleep for pagan Gods,
So, with a gracious and firm hand, Youthfulness
Poured pleasure and drunkenness for them, by turns,
    Into a vermillion goblet.

VIII

One evening, by moonlight, they sailed at will
On the star-reflected waves where Venice bathed;
They sailed and already, fading behind them, were
Masques, flames, palaces, women, flowers, a
        sonorous ball...
A love song, at a distance, barely still disturbed
    The divine silence of the skies.

IX

They had for shelter, on their fresh nights,
A white satin baldaquin with silver fringes,
Of ample and heavy folds. An antique cloak
Was extended widely over ermine cushions
And, while they dreamt to the sound of mandolins,
    Its brocaded edges trailed in the water.

X

Hermosa then said: "Lord Juan, you sigh!" –
"Yes, I suffer," he said; "but one of your smiles
Effaces my chagrins." – "You, so young and so
        handsome,
You talk of sorrows?" – "Perhaps." A long silence...
– "But my head on your chest ought to calm your
        sufferings, yes?" –
   "It is but a flower on a tomb!"

XI

She immediately added, in a gentle and grave tone of
        voice:
"Friend! You do not like your slave's songs?
Say? My cedarwood gusle[8] has the gift of charming
The miserable, perhaps?" – "Hermosa, don't. Lay off
The gusle! Nothing can console my sadnesses,
   And I admire you without loving you!"

XII

"Oh! would it be farewell already, Don Juan?" –
        "Stay!
For my last hope has left me just now;
For I want to lay my head on your bosom!
Stay! For I am the exile whom one desires;
Stay! For your beauty invites me to love,
   Me who no longer loves anything anymore!"

---

[8]gusle: from French "guzle," a musical instrument with one string.

XIII

"O, my young sultan," she responded. "You love me!
Let's exchange then two supreme riches,
That we can both dispose of immediately.
Love, I entreat you!" – "Child! what do you mean to
          say?" –
"Your soul and your sorrow, to start with, for a
          smile;
     And your secret for a kiss!"

XIV

"My secret, young lady?" he shuddered. – "My
          lips,"
She said, "can give pleasure and kindle a fever!
My velvet kisses cause torture! My hair,
With its penetrating perfumes, inebriates! My breath
Makes faint!... And, like a Siren, I can make
     You die for love! If I wanted to.

XV

"At least, that is what you have told me, dear lord!
          Your memory
Ought well to remember all this story.
Ah well, my handsome friend! If, it is true, however,
If I can give so many ineffable deliriums,
A single kiss, one sole smile,
     Is worth my lover's secret."

XVI

"What secret are you talking about, my pretty
           queen?" –
"Listen: it was in the ebony hall,
At the palace the other night; the banquet's ballads
No longer evoked love, and their profane chords
Had stopped ringing out. A diaphanous light
     Was already announcing the break of day.

XVII

"Golden tassels released the heavy draperies;
Roses fell from withered crowns;
Pallid lights tinted the stained glass windows;
Myrrh escaped from amber censers
In azure spirals; on frescoes in the room
     The lights from candelabra died out.

XVIII

"Silver flasks, poignards, dice, gloves, goblets, and
           masques
Were strewn on that mosaic in capricious disorder;
Guests, sparse, slept on sofas;
Lovers of an instant whom prodigious inebriation
Had already put to sleep, overcome by fatigue,
     Stopped speaking in whispers!

XIX

"But me, who am younger and of a different nature,
Vine branches were entwined in my hair,

And my eyes, in order to close, awaited your kisses;
A black tiger skin under my lustrous haunches
Had two holes in its face, a double swarthy mark,
    Which your bullets had pierced.

XX

"They were two shots from your prompt and sure
       hand
That at the moment of danger your calm eye
       measured...
And my spirit soared towards a happy land
That you don't mention, handsome morose voyager!
Shipwrecks, duels, perils, loves... oh! I suppose
    Quite a mysterious past.

XXI

"So, I was thinking of you, in this half-sleep
Where idealism outlived the desire that slumbered...
And I believed I saw you, in the fog of days,
Wandering, sometimes in those mountains bordering
       the clouds
That rise, over there, from unknown plains
    That one does not always return to;

XXII

"Sometimes with Arabs, with their caravans
In burning deserts; sometimes in savannahs
Where the lion bounds, his prey in his teeth;
Sometimes, pensive, in the arms of bronzed
       mistresses,

Deflowering your lovers like so many golden flowers
    That one smells and casts to the winds;

XXIII

"Sometimes in combats, with Palikars,
At the cannons' fuse, lighting your cigars,
And with the tip of your dagger goading your horse;
Sometimes alone in the emir's harem,
Whose cruel kavehs, with dirty faces,
    Guard sandalwood doors.

XXIV

"Other times, navigating to the feverish Indies
On sacred waves, near shadowy shores,
Where sapphire-blue birds everywhere flutter;
Finally, I saw you in Venice the Beautiful,
King of all banquets, your face not revealing
    Boredom, regrets, or memories!

XXV

"But you did not come. Tired of revery,
I lifted the edge of a tapestry,
Imagining that you by chance could be there;
And I saw you among the marbled columns,
Your eye fixed, fingering with two clenched fists
    The golden blade of your poignard.

XXVI

"I watched you. A terrible anguish

In your mind seemed to darken with an invisible
      shroud
The things of the orgy with its doleful debris;
Some nameless secret lowered your somber head;
You looked at the void, impassible, in the darkness,
    Like a God of accursed feasts.

XXVII

"Oh! I do not know how this thought came to me,
That you wanted to die! But it froze me.
Your boredom was not like him who is born
Of vulgar disgusts: a supreme sadness
Consecrated your pride; like a black diadem,
    The despair crowned you.

XXVIII

"And I understood then that our passionate pleasures
Could not appease your soul's ardors;
That your polite laugh, like a steel masque,
Hid a purpose that no one guesses, that nothing
      changes,
Broad, immense, frightening, impenetrable, strange...
    Am I right, handsome adventurer?"

XXIX

She had spoken, and resumed her pose of indolence.
Don Juan looked at her for some time in silence...
The winds, full of perfumes and vague chords,
Caressed their hair. "My secret? It's my life!
There is no point in bringing that up again!" – "I beg

you!" –
"Well," he said, "Then listen!

XXX

"Since I am the voice that sings to young women
In woods, on lakes, under blossoming arbors,
Unknown, powerful, and singular rhythms;
Since, sylph or genius, with magnetic wings,
I am he who comes to whisper beside them
    Oaths so easily forgotten;

XXXI

"Since, tired of living while despising life,
I gaze on death without hatred or envy,
Like a supreme shadow where lovers sleep;
Since that vengeful God, whom I am the victim of,
Has, tomorrow perhaps, in the Book of the Abyss,
    Marked the end of my days.

XXXII

"Since the autumn evening and its white light
Silvers the facades of centenarian palaces,
And since, before your beauty, I have prostrated
      myself;
Since I admire, finally, the imperial dream
Of the human aesthetic in your serene splendor;
    Since a child has divined me,

XXXIII

"From this heart filled with ecstasy, I want to
Let it escape suddenly, – the ideal that oppresses it!
Do you smell the orange trees and the magnolias?
Lift your divine eyes and listen! The hour strikes,
The hour of sensual pleasures! Shadows surround us,
    O my beauty, do not tremble!

XXXIV

"Observe well! Two nights dispute over the earth:
The one, the ball's banner, the other, a vast shroud.
Hear the noisy song of feasts,
Laughter, craziness, and sweet music!
Isn't it true that the winds of the Adriatic Gulf
    Sound like distant kisses?

XXXV

"See the innumerable lusters and the halls filled
With amorous masks, bedazzled women!
Night of humanity despairing of a God;
But lift up your face, and consider
The other: an immense night enveloping the earth
    In the folds of its blue shroud!

XXXVI

"Ah well! Beings born of man and woman,
With a fear of nothingness, wondering if they have a
        soul,
Standing before it, have understood the tomb's

> *beyond.*

The slave in oblivion, the powerful at parties,
Have said to themselves, seeing extend over their
      heads
   The terrible night and without a torch:

XXXVII

"Peace of the natal hearth! Honor, a fragile treasure!
Power, vacillating on a clay throne!
Prayer, a lowly happiness! Glory, a bleeding
      pleasure!
You, science, a word full of unfathomable empty
      spaces!
There, the vanities of our miserable destinies:
   Our only purpose is to die!

XXXVIII

"In this way, in several months, you must return to
      ashes;
Your beautiful eyes will be extinguished; alone, you
      will need to descend
The frozen spiral with its lost meanderings.
You shiver in my arms, my condemned, pale woman!
What good is it! It is the law of our destiny.
   It is, quite simply, no longer to exist.

XXXIX

"You speak of countries. What do I care about suns,
Worlds, winters, sands, and waves!
My dream is to be *over there*! You speak of dangers?

They are my only friends; and as for my face,
Do you really believe that, after the storm,
>   one might read in their faces
> The terror of sailors?

XL

"Just like the pilgrim, come in from the storm,
Telling him who departs on distant voyages
Stories of the desert with its redoubted aspects,
I wish, while waiting for death to devastate us,
First to retrace for you a vast enough spectacle...
> The desert of realities!

XLI

"August Liberty was the unique goddess
Of our first ancestors; but, endlessly more numerous,
They soon wanted different acts.
Their Liberties then fought for the palm,
And from the implacable shock when everything
>   collided,
> Tyrants were born suddenly.

XLII

"Oh! I am satisfied, from this point of view,
Of their ancient combats: my youth is endowed with
The Useful and the Beautiful, I am a son of
>   conquerors!
I march free and proud on conquered beaches;
Pleasure has shaken loose its most exquisite flowers
> For my most mocking disdains.

XLIII

"And this very evening even, if your stern beauty
Deigned not to console my haughty grief,
I would go to my seraglio in the gardens of Lemnos:
I am more than a king there; one hundred Greek
            slaves
Would pour drunkenness for me, into my silver
            goblet,
    From the wines of Cyprus and Samos!

XLIV

"I would feel grand. I have calm passions.
At twenty years old I culled myrtles and palms.
And I have known, like another, how to inspire fear.
Glory? Yes! I have known this antique statue,
Which for heroes alone becomes a woman: she
            murders,
    And she is not as beautiful as you.

XLV

"When the wind swelled my black vessel's sails,
Abed on the upper desk, dreamer, under the stars,
While the sailors slept on the bridge,
I have often seen shining in the somber wake
This phantom with its loves full of mystery and
            darkness
    Who called me from amidst the waves.

XLVI

"If the sky struck the ocean so that it rose up,
I was indifferent. Alone, deep in my dream,
I saw laurels growing in the deserts:
Brass fanfares swept away, in their death rattles,
The tempest, the ocean swell, and the deafening blasts
    Of cries of the wind and the sound of the seas.

XLVII

"On reawakening, I was a king. Brilliant banners,
Prestige, chariots, flowers, *bayaderes*,
Negroes escorted me; – fantastic frolics! –
And innumerable voices, by thunderous displays,
Cried: 'Glory to him who carries the trophies!
    Glory to the young man of combats!'

XLVIII

"That was Asia, with its strength which I admire,
Fastening round its brown flanks its cashmere
            loincloth,
With its fantasy of rainbow colors,
Its impure pariahs, its grandiose forests,
Its crops of maize and its crops of roses,
    And its beliefs without altar.

XLIX

"Yes! I have dictated laws to all those peoples.
Their frontiers, their fields, their cities, their burgs,
They wait for me, and I can pick up where I left off.

The chief of a thousand tribes whose old warriors
I can turn, in a word, from yesterday's vanquished
   Into the oppressors of tomorrow.

L

"Others have done it! – Long ago, the annals tell how
A prince, an extremely young man, a master of mares,
Lived in that country, with its profound language,
That one calls Greece. He loved the athletes,
Quadrigae, bows, chases, and feasts
   Of his harsh and fecund realm!

LI

"He had for a master a sage among sages...
He marched before him. – Victories and carnages! –
The terrified world paid him its tribute.
The satraps fled. He, during his febrile nights,
In the red glow of orgies, set towns on fire...
   He was a God. – Then he died.

LII

"A God? – To efface his sublime footprints,
Six hundred thousand victims were needed again!
– When did Alexander pass, when Darius?
– Things have regained their eternal places:
Waves in the Granicus, grasses in the Arbelles,
   And sands on the plains of Issus.

LIII

"Thus I will no longer return to the marbled steppes
Of the magic Orient. The sacred battles
Of peoples and kings may rage yet again;
But never, on elephant, will my sword or my
          cuirasses
Blind from afar the onager with his hardy loins
    Mottled by blood and gold.

LIV

"Blood for oblivion!... Wild laws of the earth!...
If at least I was alone!... Without seeing, in the dust,
The vanquished writhe under revolting yokes!...
Of course, it is noble and fine to wish for; but, in sum,
A work produced by the will of one man
    Can it last very long?

LV

"Do you know what effect a martyr of genius
Like Francois Xavier, after twenty years of agony,
Obtains after his death? – A rajah showed me
His Gods' temples, and, on an immense dome,
The breezes rocked, at the end of a gallows,
    The last Christian who remained...

LVI

"And so on and so forth, alas! – One sees, by
          intervals,
Misery, Famine, trivial sorrows,

Haggard Malady with green limbs;
Pangs of Thirst which desiccate the entrails;
Cold, breaking the teeth, within four walls,
    Under winter's harsh North wind... –

LVII

"Fatalities! – With the milk of their wet nurses
The living have sucked from all those bitter
        chalices!...
So much so that the gall of a suffering breast
Bears the same name, braids the same fibers
As the gentle and strong juice drunk by free children
    At the free breast they have emptied.

LVIII

"Snatch from Misfortune those desolate races,
Reanimate today those immolated castes? –
To do it again tomorrow. Too late! – I'm not keen
        on that.
Then, and it hurts to say it, one more thing:
Fortune demeans the poor people of yesterday!
    They haven't got much beside their mean beds!

LIX

"Oh! Not wishing to judge or despise anyone,
I do not know how to hate! I complain, or I pardon.
Far be it from me to outrage the poor, verily!
A prey to heavy rags, when his body cracks and
        bends,
That one there is great, who is scoffed at and

despoiled.
Opprobrium is a majesty!

LX

"Lugubrious matters! – Often, to distract myself,
I changed the adverse Fortune of several people.
They were proud and pure: they complained amongst
        themselves...
But as soon as a little gold blinded their sunken eyes,
They were pitiless with their fellow slaves;
        Their egoism was hideous.

LXI

"You can give alms with such a smile
That, if I were a poor fellow, for me it would
        suffice!...
Almsgiving suits you so well! In this act, especially,
I will love, in your arms, a wearier languor,
A curve drawn with such a humble grace...
        What else is there, after all?

LXII

"Old Cain! You drank your fratricidal tears
When thirst first seized you in your torrid sands;
But when the rain finally came pouring down,
You could see in the sunlight, on drenched earth,
Under its hair glistening with dew drops,
        Your glistening tiger skin!

LXIII

"If Fate deprived you of Eden and its charms,
You knew the taste of tears, son of tears!
It must be like this for all modern Cains.
Let them, revolted, be conquerors! My tomb is ready:
And I know how to die with the same attitude
    That I toss my purse full of sequins to them!

LXIV

"And you yourself, Hermosa, when up against time,
Under the jealous breath of the irritated Parca,
If you saw the sidereal nimbus fade away
From your head, you too would say, in your stoical
            pride,
The simply true words of that ancient queen:
    'The dagger does no harm!'

LXV

"Am I right?" – She was silent and serious;
And Don Juan's bright eyes observed on her face
The effect that his voice had produced in her heart.
The lamp, at the rudder, shined on the pale waves,
But the lily-white splendors of Hermosa's traits
    Grew dark like the night.

LXVI

Just as, in elevated glaciers where the snow sparkles,
The pure crystal of a lake conceals from curious
            hunters

The unknown dangers in its calmness:
When a downpour suddenly lets loose and passes,
One sees mounting to the surface mysterious indices
   from the sand bed.

LXVII

"O you whom I gaze on and whom I find beautiful,
You tremble?" – "Beloved prince, keep talking!" she
   said:
"And when your love of the poor and humanity,
When hope and glory with your faith in God
Have deserted your heart, what remains?" – "What
   remains
  Is a phantom: Voluptuousness!

LXVIII

"Since you have chosen it, since it is your emblem,
Do you want to see, in a single instant, its ultimate
   limit?
Let's evoke a mortal who could wear
Like a glaring symbol of all human labor
The headband of Isis, the Roman sandal,
  And the purple cloak of Tyre!

LXIX

"The Emperor Tiberius, exiled on the Isle of Capri! –
Ah! now that was a guest at the gilded table
Of the terrestrial elect: his peerless throne
Looked down on three rows of vexillary guards;
He saw the eagle shine from his galleys

On the waves, in the fire of the sun!

LXX

"Somber practitioner of the most occult spasms,
When his nerves, made languid by horrible
          marasmuses,
Resisted... He loved, he did, that triumphal Caesar,
The obscure voluptuousness of bloody inebriations,
He felt impotent furies rise up in himself
     With a jackal's instincts.

LXXI

"His lictors escorted him in Rome. He was master.
His tunic was fragrant with cinnamon, maybe;
But if someone murmured, he extended his hand;
And with a derisive scepter, prefiguring his revenge,
He sinisterly made the two hundred hoary heads
     Of old men in the Roman Senate bow.

LXXII

"Let's cover his sickly body with the most beautiful
          shapes;
That bronze muscles might rest on his frail members,
That his deformed rictus might hold a friendly smile,
That a strong and pure timbre might replace his
          raucous voice,
That fire might be rekindled at the back of his
          glaucous eye;
     That youth might be upon him!

LXXIII

"And that on his beauty there might be the
          diaphanous taint
Of Endymion, then when chaste Diana, –
Under the odoriferous shade of a thick *alisier*,
Under the moon beams, and on the argentine sward,
Finding him asleep next to an enchanted stream, –
     Woke him with a kiss.

LXXIV

"That Study now, with its silent bitternesses,
Might condense its antique volumes to its call;
That it might recognize the intimate relationships of
          laws;
That for it the science of the priests of Memphis,
Of the magicians of Ecbatana, forbidden to the
          profane,
     Might hand over the key to their treasures.

LXXV

"That he might know the secrets of old anchorites
When, alone at their discreet cisterns in the deserts,
They watch the stars march across the sky,
And when, lowering their foreheads inundated with
          light,
They die, leaving the care for their dust
     To mysterious north winds.

LXXVI

"That he might have in his power, if all turns insipid
          for him,
The philters that revive his deteriorating body;
The beverages of the sultans of fabulous excesses;
The Elixirs of Hermes of ancient Chaldea,
Known perhaps in subterranean India,
     Whose caves have no point of access.

LXXVII

"For there are fakirs in those carved-out retreats,
Dreams of an Arab tale with marvelous lamps,
Old, funereal and naked, in their mysticity;
Inflexible in science and shadow and wonders!
What's become of the dead? No one knows. – No
          traces!...
     As if they had never existed.

LXXVIII

"And if there are not enough Italian villas
To house this man and his immense life,
That the old world might pile up in monstrous heaps
Its hanging gardens, its gold or alabaster blocks,
Its circuses of Titans and its amphitheaters,
     In a vertiginous palace!

LXXIX

"That he might scrutinize at leisure the details, the
          nuances

Of depravations with their subtle essences!
In the lustral wave, to the sound of charming lutes,
Pictures of delirium and antique debauchery
Garlanded around a portico's pillars, shuddering, –
    That they might come back to life for him!

LXXX

"And, like the Libyan Phoenix of pyres,
Reborn from its ashes and purified,
That Pleasure, the victor of saddened disgusts,
Immortal holocaust, might be reborn, new again,
From its own boredoms! That it might be young,
        continually,
    For one hundred years of voluptuousness!

LXXXI

"That his all-powerful vows might be content within
        the boundaries that
The world has restrained his mournful delights to!
That he might be the name made flesh of all human
        desire,
That, insensible to the aspect of asylum which
        everything devolves to,
He might have no conception of the tomb's trances,
    And that he might find himself *happy*, at last!"

LXXXII

– "Is that it?" – "Yes, that is it. Of course, at this late
        hour,
If he has not wished for a better existence,

Celestial lightning flashes will have furrowed
His nights, and flowers finely scented his dawns;
And Glory will come, with its sonorous hymns,
    Like a God to surround him!

LXXXIII

"But, on the edge of the grave, he will tell himself:
     'Glory,
A flower in profound daylight, a lightning bolt in
     black night,
Vanities! What good are they, all that dazzle,
All those things one must love and feel sorry for,
If the flower must wither and the lightning bolt
     disappear...
    If, finally, man must die?'

LXXXIV

"O death! Stupor! Nothingness! A sad door that opens
Over unknown skies whose abyss covers us,
Or devouring sleep that is not recovered from!
Why be born under its power if it is an evil?
Why fear it if it is our deliverance?
    O somber scepter of the beyond!

LXXXV

"Tenebraes! The response is a God, says the priest;
The sage says: 'Back!' and the man says: 'Perhaps!'
Three words! The yawning Sphinx alone remains
     defined.
You can clearly see two nights disputing over the

    earth:
The one is nothing but life, or Fortune, or Misery;
    The other is an infinite Problem!"

LXXXVI

And their barque drifted. The waves, in the shadows,
Broke against the heavy oars with deaf clamors;
And the ebony prow where the gondolier sleeps,
Curled up over the water; harmonious voices
Accorded in the distance, in the carved-out lagoons
    Where the moon came to shine.

LXXXVII

But they didn't hear the barcarolles' song!
Hermosa had lost herself in his words;
She remembered things from bygone days;
And looking at him who had possessed her:
"By what past is your soul preceded?"
    She said, finally, in a faint voice.

LXXXVIII

Don Juan answered her: "My twenty-seventh year
Furrows its spontaneous wrinkle between my brows.
However, I still love those memories of the sky,
Those days when my blessed childhood, tanned
By the sun, I raced over the blooming fields,
    In the great woods by the old castle.

LXXXIX

"The girls in the vicinity, children with pure faces,
Had already come to play in the wild copses.
They came to play, the girls from the manors,
Beside the pale orphan. And, at times, under the
       willows,
The breezes made my curly black hair
    Float over their white shoulders.

XC

"Then, sixteen! The golden age!... Noisy serenades;
Duels under balconies at the corner of arcades;
Playing dice and the guitar with its turbulent accords;
Wine pitchers broken against a dive's plastered walls;
The mask, the cloak, the felt hat with a red feather in
      it...
    How happy I was then!

XCI

"They still remember me over there: young girls
Believe they see me in the misty Castille brushwood;
My name is like that of ephemeral demons;
The guardians of flocks sing, on their demesnes,
Your ballade, O Don Juan, beside the fire on the
      plains,
    To a group of shepherds huddled around.

XCII

"To live in my manor; to quit adventures;

To keep, insouciant, useless armors;
To be a cold spectator of this vast universe;
To see altars crumble or armies perish,
Or thrones battle to the laughter of pygmies?...
  I had other dreams in my heart.

XCIII

"I was a prince, after all; I made use of my youth
And I marched, joyous, from mistress to mistress.
At first, I sought only love and sensual delights;
Then, at the vexing hour when the body retires,
I thought I saw disgust at the bottom of everything...
  I was tired of realities.

XCIV

"To hang a silk ladder from golden trellises;
To love a *fille de joie* in a tavern;
Bah! pearls and stones, insipid boredoms.
No longer able to love like common people,
I conceived of an august and solitary desire:
  It alone made me what I am.

XCV

"It alone made me brave the Gods and tempests.
It alone made me love the sounds of conquest;
By it, my wandering steps of exploits are illustrated.
Because of it, through appalling dramas,
I have made more than a thousand women throb
  In my desperate arms.

XCVI

"Heroes have one goal only: they think on it without
        cease;
The painter has his painting; the poet, his dream;
The conqueror, his glory, and the priest, his law.
Always discovering therein new profundities,
They have a vague hope of immortal beauties.
        Man has need of a little faith.

XCVII

"Ah, well, that feeling that torments without respite,
That accursed ideal, the unknown, that dream
Before which humans succumb one after the other,
That hope, which some look for in science,
Others in faith, and still others in power,
        Me, I looked for it in love.

XCVIII

"Love, it is the absolute. By its poignant joy,
A kiss given in response to a kiss electrifies me.
Like a divine lightning bolt in the darkness of my
        heart,
It rocks a sort of deep chasm in me
Where creation unveils itself, sublime,
        In an interior spectacle.

XCIX

"Yes! I wanted to know from each creature
If that word, which twitches at the very heart of our

nature,
Had a hidden meaning unknown on earth.
I saw quite strange girls stammering.
I knew tombs where angels foundered...
     Those are the traces of my steps.

C

"Cloisters isolated in the depth of the wood, on hills,
You remember well, over there, in your ruins,
The nocturnal knight with dreadful regrets.
Ah! The hour of love is the hour of phantoms;
Your nuns chanted it in their lugubrious psalms...
     Their songs stifle their sighs.

CI

"O river of forgetfulness! With your friendly waves,
Fill my golden cup, for pale virgins,
While expiring, have not at all achieved their secret;
And when the moon shines on the alabaster and ivy,
Caressing with its rays their cinerary urns,
     The wind moans in the forest.

CII

"Countless loves! Through lands
Where a fiery air weighs on bronze-colored children,
I came, djinn or king, carried by the simoon.
Nothing could sate the strange thirst in my heart.
Finally, I reflected on myself like an archangel
     Suddenly precipitated.

CIII

"I saw, in the East, a black nation
Surround an idol with an ivory face:
That troop marched in single file for a long time at its
          feet;
Women, with gloomy cries, brandished
Torches made of red cypress, in the shadows...
     The god remained grave and mute.

CIV

"Well, I found myself like that idol.
The torches made a wild aureole;
Those endless visions that passed under my eyes,
Ah! They were my lovers! Don't you see, O my love;
They were burying themselves in eternal night,
     Offering up their farewell songs to me.

CV

"'Alone' – That word enlightened me like a
          conscience.
So much glory, bereavement, struggles, power
For some memories of vain sensual delights!
A thought then ran through my entire being:
A person loses himself in the many! one suffices
          perhaps...
     – O mortal obscurities!

CVI

"Do not sages have this grandiose law:

– 'Focus your happiness on one thing only!' –
For Daedalus, just one seraglio! Why keep changing?
I looked for your child, your masterpiece, O nature,
In order to recreate its simple and pure soul
    From the soul of my lovers!

CVII

"Hermosa, do you think that in Spain
I cannot recognize detours in the mountains?
Do you believe it was only by chance that I found
      you?
Hermosa, I was waiting for the supreme moment
When a woman is flustered by these words: 'I love
      you!'
    And watched over you from a distance.

CVIII

"Poverty, that somber skeleton with fatal eyes
That, in the evening, tramples under foot the celestial
      crowns
Of sixteen-year-old virgins, was about to consume
      you.
I needed to isolate you from those morose spheres,
To trim the thorns off your bouquet of roses,
    O you whom I wished to love!

CIX

"Look! The satin lilacs embroidered with chrysoprase
Covers your nacreous body with naïve ecstasies,
And that silver tulle nuances your comely bosom;

Slaves, flowers, perfumes, lusters, hair, riches,
Frame your beauty, your loves, your youth
   In your Venetian palace.

CX

"And everything that I sense of ardent sympathies,
Of kisses wherein one believes his numbed lips
Under golden effluvia, which are disheveled
By languors in the midst of pleasures and fecund
      mysteries,
Of enervating spasms, and of profound delights, –
   I constructed your soul out of that.

CXI

"Don't you have the beauty that, in insomnias,
Makes believe in the ideal of infinite loves?
But at that ideal my heart must stop.
Too late! it can no longer contain its thought.
Ah! would that someone might explain to me this
      insane phrase:
   'Too late! I can no longer love.'

CXII

"I can no longer love, do you understand, young lady!
Burnt like Cain by an invisible flame,
I'm thirsty for a paradise I've been exiled from.
To live means nothing to me anymore: I am tired of
      myself.
My heart, deaf sepulcher, retains only blasphemy
   For that beautiful heaven forever veiled.

CXIII

"Yes! if you exist in the ineffable spheres,
Lord, you have made things formidable.
You have made the sons of grief doubt;
You have made your sublime stars shine
In the eyes of executioners, as in their victims' eyes,
    You have made that, Lord."

CXIV

Like the dark Spirit that keeps a watch over suicides,
Don Juan stood up clenching his livid fists.
His eyes had a lethal and superhuman flash to them:
But Doubt broke the flight of his djinn,
And, seeing Hermosa pale and as if grown somber,
    Don Juan kissed her divine forehead.

CXV

Like a great sparrowhawk in the ether that hovers
Over its frightened white prey, a dove:
A lead shot whistles and hits it, its flight will
        straighten,
It falls, and it covers still with the shadows of its
        wings
The lowly bird entranced by its black pupils;
    It swoops down on it to die.

CXVI

"Yes! I am thirsty. The ancients called me Tantalus;
And, better than hetaera for the imperial soul,

Without being fatigued, I am unappeased.
The Impossible is a specter sitting beside my bed.
But, what can I say, Hermosa! Let your beautiful
            mouth
      Smile at my ravished kiss!"

CXVII

They spoke softly. In the nocturnal fog
The palace, on the waves, rose taciturnly;
The portico opened: They had returned.
Nothing seemed to have changed on their noble faces.
By degrees, torches and pages hastened round them
      And everything closed up behind them.

CXVIII

For those whom they had invited to their royal
            parties,
They were just two young people, insouciant and
            pale;
Sadly, they hardly exchanged a glance
Sometimes. One fine day, Don Juan said, "O my
            beautiful!
I am leaving you." – "Friend, it's okay," she said,
      In response to her lover.

CXIX

She added, pensively, "And the Bohemian woman
Who foretold your death at the hour of mine?"
But Don Juan just smiled down at her from among his
            lovers!

The following morning, without tears, they said to
      each other:
"Adieu!" In a kiss, their hearts united
    With this word: "Forever."

CXX

When her first lover leaves her, what a rude shock
For a woman! – boredom, disgusts, and solitude!...
Her most rich bouquet has forever withered:
Another lover soon makes her forget, doubtless,
But can she ever regain her way
    And get back again what she gave?

Song the Third: Compassion

I

Muse, what an admirable and rare privilege!
By instinct, she shrugged her shoulders white as snow
Before all that life offers with its impure *ennuis*;
Like a statue of sovereign forms, she accepted,
With a withering smile the human miseries
    And sorrows of obscure days.

II

Anguish and terrors had rocked her before:
As for solitude, she was weary of it;
Our vain words, sorrows, sufferings, regrets,
Brushed her without leaving any more of a trace
Than a flight of vultures leaves on the surface

Of the Ocean with its dark secrets.

III

She was not one of those vulgar souls
That nothing can offend and who hardly feel a thing:
The prince had unwittingly, each day, gently
Decorated and polished the least advantages
Of her mind made of savage elegances,
    As one cuts a diamond;

IV

And his influence had affected her, besides.
When he wanted to speak, his expression and his
          gestures
Emphatically articulated his disdainful terms.
Hermosa listened to him, and her exquisite nature
Was lifted, until, submissive by degrees,
    Everything was seen through his eyes.

V

Ah! daughter of the bandit, comely profane virgin,
How perfectly conscious you were of your arms of a
          courtesan
Extending from then on to embrace your universe!
How your heart leapt, in your hard breast,
When you understood finally that all nature
    Gave itself to your bitter kisses!

VI

Yes, like the shirt of Deianira,[9]
The past burned you; but before your empire
You suddenly seized it in its innermost fold;
And, clenching your white fingers on your unfeeling
         torso,
You tore it off in a single swipe and threw it, calmly,
     Into the deaf dungeons of forgetfulness.

VII

A single purpose guided her life from then on:
To drain by long draughts the cups of ambrosia,
Unbridled deliriums, generous helpings of
         sensuality.
Not to seek in love any other hope
Than that of pleasure, and to cut herself silently off
     From the rest of reality.

VIII

Even in the shaking arms of the spasm oppressing
         her,
To smile, impenetrable and cold enchantress!
To receive kisses, but never to give them;
To love for herself only and never to give up her soul,
To consider herself, for all that, above all blame,
     To die young and in a palace;

---

[9]shirt of Deianira: In reference to the poisoned shirt that Deianira
gave to her husband, Hercules.

IX

That was her dream! Then, with her graceful hands,
Without wasting precious hours in sadness,
Bidding as if a final farewell to fine days,
She entered the world wearing her diadem
Of incredible beauty, the master of herself,
    Calm, under burning gazes.

X

– And her multiple lovers? There was one reason for
        them:
Her complete loss of admiration for everything.
One man alone must never again fill her wounded
        heart
Nor suffice to fill the emptiness of her soul...
Who could fully satisfy a woman
    Who has Don Juan in her past?

XI

She loved to change lovers, the beautiful girl!
This was hardly Laïs, scoffing and squandering,
Nor Circe, exhausting men with irritating disdains,
Nor Danae either: her triumphal parties
Were always simple; and as for venal matters –
    She knew how to smile at times.

XII

When, to arouse the languor that reposes,
She moved the folds of her pink mouth

With a certain emotional expression replete with
       lascivious pleasures,
And when her lovers, taken with immediate
       paleness,
Faltered at her feet, mad with boundless love,
    And shivers, and desires;

XIII

Then she abandoned herself voluntarily, with
       lethargy,
To the sensual disturbances of a night of youth;
But, if they hoped for a more perfect love from her,
If they expected a soul they could dedicate their lives
       to...
A mask of silence and polished glass
    Smiled at them on first mention.

XIV

Did she not know that an entire existence
Of joy or sorrows, hate or hope,
Depends on the memory of deflowered dreams?
That if it tarnishes the sky of our first loves,
It sadly casts its doleful shadows
    On the destinies it has damned?

XV

Ah! Don Juan loved all those young mothers
Who wept after him for their ephemeral joys.
Disasters and tombs! He passed on indomitable;
He chatted; he opened himself up to their faithful

souls...
And if for him they were phantoms, for them
    He remained a reality.

XVI

Now, well understanding that a single man could not
      satisfy
Nor dominate her life, she preferred to be silent.
Guarding her freedom as one guards a treasure,
She had no desire for more tender expansion...
How they must have suffered by failing to understand
      her
    And seeing her change again!

XVII

To be sure, she took after the ancient Aspasia,
The real Astarte, goddess of Attica.
I admire that woman with the solid advice
Who knew how to entertain, on Olympiad nights,
Socrates, Pericles, Phidias, Alcibiades,
    And to remain a goddess on re-awakening.

XVIII

Also, far from the ducal salons of Italy,
The greatest men under heaven composed her chosen
      court;
And by the grace of I don't know what delicious tact,
Painters, musicians, savants, sculptors, poets
Found themselves, each time they left her parties,
    Greater, prouder, happier.

XIX

O glittering evenings! The porphyry vases,
Flames and flowers, fresh bursts of laughter,
Ingenuous pages with their white liveries,
Streams of silk and gold; the pretty brown-haired girls
On the arms of their young men, in the shadows
     of the lagoons,
  Descending a great flight of stairs!

XX

O Venice! today those things are dead!
The black eagles of Austria and its pale cohorts
Clamp their foot on you, noble daughter of the seas.
Your valiant liberty laughed to see its scented sash
Floating over the laurels of yesteryear:
  Instead of flowers, why the irons?

XXI

In the past, you were seen in all your riches!
You slept on your lightning, like a goddess:
And your vessels sailed unimpeded on their journeys:
Your double renown filled history with wonder:
Foreigners were excited by your stories of glory,
  As by your love stories.

XXII

O Venice! O power! O dust! All things pass.
Your children loved them, those romances by Tasso
Under the marble arches with the faded echos...

But your glory is forgotten, and, on their brown
      waves,
In the evening, meandering through the lagoons,
   Your gondoliers no longer sing!

XXIII

– But sometimes the doleful and pale idler,
Enervated by triumphs, balls, and lust,
Withdrew all alone into her concerned mourning;
Anxiety hovered over her melancholy,
She felt rolling down her pallid cheek
   The moving tears of her young beaus.

XXIV

She then picked up her harp with its deep chords
And, with her fingers, struck in smooth preludes
The harmony of a *canzone* to an oriental rhythm:
The winged arpeggio vibrated, and the musician
Softly raised her Aeolian voice,
   Her crystal-timbered voice.

XXV

She returned quickly to sumptuous battles!
The voluptuous flowers of midnight bouquets
Dropped their petals on her bed with dazzling
      splendor;
And like the Spartan boy's fox,
Pleasure, without leaving a visible trace,
   Silently gnawed at her white breast.

XXVI

Two years had passed in this insalubrious air
That spoils and kills; a lugubrious malaise
Seized her suddenly; it was common law.
Ecstasy broke her, too long contained.
She heard Death, in the intervening shadow,
     Whispering into her ear: "It's me." –

XXVII

"Already!" she said. "Ah, well, the angel of terror
Can come: I've lived, I wait, I'm content.
Farewell waves and countries where Voluptuousness
          sleeps!
I'd like to say just one more thing:
Look! I die young and that consoles me,
     At least I die in my beauty."

Preludes

A Manner of Imitating M. de Pompignan

Impotent cries! Bizarre furors!
All the while these barbarous monsters...

– M. LE FRANC DE POMPIGNAN

(In response to toasts and English journals: July, 1858.)

Englishmen, you have done despicable things:
You have insulted, by reprehensible words,
A flag that you have trembled before, all of you.
Come on, in truth, these things are cowardly:
Look through its noble folds to find the marks:
    You will find nothing there but bullet holes.

The flag of a country, it is the country itself.
Ours is the shroud and emblem of heroes,
The restraint of foreigners and honor of the soldier.
It is the dead ancestors watching in the shadows,
It is the standing altar delivered of a somber yoke;
    It is our heart that beats, finally.

At all times in the past, under its beloved colors,
It made honor wave in front of our troops.
It could be vanquished at times, but it never faded;

And when someone comes forward to challenge its
      valiance,
Our old standard is deployed in silence
    And signals the cannons that respond for it.

The veritable name that is borne, in life, by
Bourbon, Napoleon, Valois, it is the Fatherland.
What difference does the flag's color make to great
      countries?
Eagle or golden *fleurs-de-lys*, that is a matter of the
      times;
Those enemy heroes, brothers by their courage, –
    God reunites them in the grave.

Why these vain defiances, these insensate clamors?
We know how to ignore many things of the past.
History should be let alone in its shroud of horror.
What's the point of stirring the common dust?
Oh! don't keep bragging to us about your parents'
      crime:
    A jailor's opprobrium in the face of an emperor.

Given that he reposes now at the edge of the Seine,
Lower your voices, Englishmen of Saint Helen,
Your voices of belated courage. Don't wake him;
Don't wake him in his great stone bed.
France is sometimes too near to England...
    Englishmen, Englishmen, lower your voices!

Envoi

    A sword reposes beside a bier:
    We must wait for him to repossess it;

A throne, for him who dreams, –
A throne is quite somber these days!
The pinnacle of human vanity,
At its feet many hatreds bleed;
Often it covers one's suffering!
An obscure crowd waits at the threshold:
A fir tree covered with white ermine,
It has a scepter and laurels for branches:
It is constructed of four planks
Absolutely just like a coffin.

Divine Nature

The hawthorn has blossomed on the green hillocks;
The morning wind, in the deserted plains,
Half opens the night's roses, while bending them;
The night's roses, like areoles,
Incline their corollas alongside the dark bushes;
And at their feet, in the grass, the bluet fades.
The bush hides from the sky and rain and dawn
The bluet that withers and that thirst devours.
The night's roses, how well they know it!
Thus, seeming to bend to the murmur
Of the butterfly-zephyrs, their Don Juans of morning,
They have a distracted look for its verdure:
And this look is enough for it to live, O Nature!
For it allows a tear to fall, a pure drop of water,
        That quenches it until tomorrow.

Yesterday Evening

"You rehash each evening all those morose thoughts:
Do they know the Lord's secret better than you do?
Is it better to contemplate men and things
    Than to come away with me?

"Glory, you know, is but a wisp of smoke;
Myrtles, my friend, are irrigated with tears:
Instead, come into my shade, with your sweetheart!
    In the shade you will uncover flowers still."

– And me, I smiled to see her so pretty.
I felt so much joy that I was shaking all over;
Then I took her hand, her dear pale hand,
    And I softly kissed it.

Spring

Here are the first days of spring and shade,
    Already the sweet birds sing;
And melancholy inhabits the foliage:
Temperate breezes blow in the copse,
    And make the streams ripple.

And the gentle concerts that spring restores
    With its rays and its flowers;
The bellowing flocks, the verdant plain,
And the white butterflies breathing the breath
    Of violets in tears;

And the new air charged with odors and life,
    The azure where a golden sun shines,
Reawakening from winter the ravished countryside,
It is all a prayer where the sky urges us
    To feel young again.

Listen to the thousand voices of immense nature;
    They speak to you in turns.
My dear, one often understands them without
       thinking about it:
The rays say to us: "God!"; and nature: "Hope!";
    And the violet: "Love!"

At Her Bedside

Often at night I come to open your closed doors:
I admire the charming languor of your poses,
Your form under the folds that hide your nakedness:
How I love to watch my lover who reposes,
    Sleeping in her beauty!

Your sleep is impressed with a graceful gentleness,
Your mouth is half open, smiling, –
Your mouth of coral! In the shadows, the small lamp
Projects a doubtful, vacillating light
    Over your friendly face.

Seeing your arms crossed under the lace, I say:
"My exiled sufferer has spread her two wings...
May her soul escape for a moment from here below,
To ideal gardens, and gather some immortelles!...

Oh! Do not waken!"

Séïd Castle

I

It was a strong castle hard by Spain,
Whose mossy crenelations were crumbling for old
            age:
One might have called it a giant, the child of somber
            mountains,
Sublime in its silence and immobility.
It rested on its plinth intertwined with ivy,
A formless group of rocks, chasms, and stones;
Mountains and rocks, – they were its pedestal;
And the snow from the sky covered in its shroud
      The feet of the colossal monster.

II

It slept or grew old. O the splendor of ruins!
The storm stood back from the old manor,
And, full of the past, dominating the hills, it
Pitted its dark exterior against the furious lightning.
From a distance, in the valleys quivering in the shade,
The sun beams tinged the green foliage with gold;
The hairy beeches sheltered the pasture;
And often in that place the wild doves warbled
      With the gentle coos of love.

III

But the manor, filled with menacing grandeur,
Guarded, like an old man, its silence and the night;
And on the broken walls of its crumbling head,
The lugubrious owl hooted from its nest.
For ramparts, it had the rocks of the Pyrenees;
For moats, the torrents; for summit, the clouds,
Where its face was lost when evening fell.
It stood up straight with its destinies,
     Calm like despair.

IV

Austere visions pass over your rubble,
Where silence speaks to the man who shivers, –
O you, somber caryatid of memories!
O castles crevassed in your walls of granite.
For the ogive writhes in mauresque spirals
On your bronze trefoils with their sculptured shapes...
And the Abbasid marble, forgotten only by time,
Stumps the contours of their oriental arms, –
     The seal of a race of giants.[10]

Dawn

The slender roe amuse themselves in the wood;
Solitude, with its myriad voices, inhabits the forests
     With their green depths;

---

[10]Original footnote: This is taken from the poem *Séïd*, which the author is working on at this moment.

And the small, satisfied flowers of the vale
Gaze up at the sky while some butterfly
    Notices their opened corollas.

To Mme. The Countess de C***

Madam, we crossed paths once;
I was very young then, and you also, I believe.
We are still young, at least in years;
They have grazed your face, surprised
To see them fly by ever so lightly:
Yours has remained charming, but mine has aged.
You are a mother now, and if the great joy
Of crumpling velvet and silk at balls,
Of kissing your children's pure faces,
Of passing over everyone with a triumphant gaze
Like a young queen finally, calm and pensive;
If plucking petals from a fugitive flower in this way,
With its sweet perfumes, which one calls happiness;
If all that makes your heart grow old, before its time,
You must begin to know life.
For me, life is another flower altogether, that no one
       wants;
Which, all alone, I culled from wayside brambles;
To get at it I had to bloody my hand:
I was only a child then, Madam, but I plucked it:
And, since then, its bitter scent has withered my soul.
I still love it though; there it is, in my heart;
Do not ever reach for it, – its name is Sorrow!

De Profundis Clamavi[11]

A Cross and oblivion, night and silence!

— ALFRED DE MUSSET

I

O charming dog roses! Sunlight, rays, verdure,
Fresh salutation that the earth offers in a murmur
By zephyrs rejuvenating hearts full of hope,
Coppices still completely full of chaste reveries,
Six months have passed, far from your cherished
     blossoms –
  I needed to see you again.

Oh! you remember, delicious forest,
That pretty child who, gracious, passed,
Smiling simply up at the sky, at the future,
Losing herself with me in the green alleys?
Ah well! among the lilies of your somber valleys,
  You will not see her come again.

O spring! O lilies! O profound leafy boughs!
As before, your flowers, so loved by her,
Exhale their loves along your deserted paths:
The hawthorn entwines around the bower's bench,
Birds sing, skies are blue, and the sun shines;
  Nothing has changed on fine days!

Silent valley! It was merely a dream,

---

[11]*De Profundis Clamavi*: Latin for "Out of the depths have I cried unto thee[, O Lord]." From Psalms 130:1. It is also the title of a poem by Baudelaire in "Spleen et Idéel" from *Les Fleurs du Mal*.

A radiant thought that has drawn to a close
And leaves a bitter memory behind...
Don't ask me what has become of her,
The poor girl who came into his world
    To console and die!...

She's dead! and I am still prey to existence!
Is this life then? And has my childhood
Already vanished far from this broken heart?
Lord, you are great, but you are severe!
And so, here I am alone: all is finished on earth;
    It is called "the Past."

II

Alas! I remember. – The breezes, in the shade,
Rippled the somber waves of the harmonious river;
The winged songs of evening vanished;
And the moon, gliding amidst the white clouds,
Often illuminated the taints of the foliage
    With the chiaroscuro of lovely nights.

The nightingale, hidden behind thick leafage,
Modulated the sighs of its exquisite canticle;
Flowers, in their sweets scents, fell asleep by and by;
And, like two rays reuniting their flame,
The two of us folded our souls into one,
    And our two hearts became one love.

How pretty her foot was, treading on the moss!
How silky and soft her hair!
We went, interlaced, under the tall poplars;
She was sixteen years old; I was almost that age.

Often the nightingale held its breath
    Listening to our soft paces.

And I contemplated my pensive lover,
And we went along, alone, near the bank,
Her hand on my shoulder, my head on her hand;
And the shivers of the solitary night
Transported to heaven, like a prayer,
    Both our dreams along the path.

III

Then, the awakening! death! a changed existence!
O Time! chilling old man! what have you done with
        my angel?
Where have you put her, alas! Cold, and forever?
What have you done with the young child filled with
        charms,
What have you done with the smile and tears,
    Oh! what have you done with our love?

IV

Look how well the flowers fare, near graves!
One would say a bouquet that young doves,
Returning to their land, have left us by way of adieu.
– What did she do then to die first?
Is it a crime to live? And love, on earth,
    Isn't it God's pardon?

Don't smile at me anymore, O immortal countryside!
I'm all alone now; if it was not for her,
I had no need of your fresh beauties.

Haven't I seen the chasm that all things fall into?
Lilies die in the shade where the roses wither:
    The cypresses alone remain standing.

She lies beneath the cypresses, the pale young
        woman!
My sad, proud love still burns in my soul,
Like a golden lamp of old, on a bier.
But, I don't weep anymore: sorrow has its charms.
And besides, O my God, my eyes have no more tears,
    And only my heart wears black mourning!

To My Friend Amédée le Menant

I

At the moment of quitting his faded childhood,
When a man suddenly sees the earth less ornate,
    The sky more unknown;
For the first time in his life reflecting on himself,
He asks himself, dreaming, a most important
        question:
    "Why am I here?"

II

Ah! poor sailor! Far from life's shores
You stop; you try to understand what route your boat
    Followed with its blue wake.
But the deafening wave carries it and endlessly leads
    it astray.
In the sea fog, Destiny, that somber beacon,

Raises a finger of light.

III

Behind him, far away, nearly at shore,
The rower already sees the images fluttering
     Across the pure and veiled faces:
A mother, a sister, his fiancée even...
Sometimes he remembers that a frozen earth
     Closes their star-filled eyes.

IV

And these are the bygone farewells: the white hands
That squeezed his hand; kisses under the branches,
     And youthful loves...
But to continue sailing alone toward long beaches,
Turning his head away, he rips out these pages
     From his journal.

V

Then there's the tempest with its mournful memories.
Tragedy, swimming next to him in the darkness,
     Follows him like a friend;
And, shutting his tired eyes, if the mariner sleeps,
Tragedy takes hold of the helm, and watches
     Over its man asleep.

VI

We must put up a good fight against man and space!
For having lost everything, in the torment that

transpires
While coursing through the skies,
So as to support the burden of shared miseries,
Instead of helping each other, all humans, these
        brothers of ours, –
    They hate each other.

VII

Some, who are indifferent, keel over in their jackets
And go away. Sometimes the boats touch one
        another...
    Two are stronger than one;
And, looking for a supreme refuge in love,
Alone, they sail in peace without dread or blasphemy,
    Toward an unsoundable port.

VIII

But he who, intrepid and tranquil, examines
The men and waves, to whom the sterile sea
    Still offers a reef,
He rises in silence and fights solitarily.
Every sail for him is a shroud fundamentally,
    Every skiff a coffin.

IX

The anchor he wishes to cast, – lightning loosens it;
Pale, finally, he grabs hold of his heart and shakes it...
    And every illusion,
Hope, friendship, charity, sublime faith
Falls around him. – To be born, is it a crime

Or a malediction? –

X

Alone then, the old man, releasing the sail,
Abandons his vessel with its broken masts
     To oblivion's waves, that starless sea...
Until the moment when, leaving one more hourglass
          to fall
To the bottom of the urn, taciturn Destiny
     In the darkness says "Enough."

XI

The wave speaks softly to the shores it brushes
          against,
And one can still hear on the weeping Ocean
     The gloomy wind that escapes;
And each dawn arrives to cast light on, O mystery!
The anxious songs of Earth's children
     Who depart for the Night!

Discouragement

And yet, far from an impure century,
Free and alone in the deserted wood,
If I could have come into the world
On the first days of the Universe;

When, over its uncovered beauty,
Eve passed her blue eyes,
When the earth was young and green,

And when man believed in God!

With accents of the sacred text
That all things newly born
Hymned under an expansive, clear sky
To their unknown Creator;

Simple and docile, I would have had hope!
For in those long-gone days,
Belief was not difficult...
But the world has changed since then.

Today we have only to follow
A path just yesterday beaten...
What is it, alas, to live now?
– To remember that one lived. –

On a Rock

Splendid was the night; the stars' reflections
Bounced on the waves, and the languid waves
Gently rocked the white sails in the distance
Like seagulls fallen asleep on the breeze.
Beneath pallid clouds, the evening star veiled
The rays sifting through its silver shadows;
Fishermen's songs, which drifted ashore
On charming waves, undulated while dying;
The swell crashed like an immense sigh,
But so softly that one could hear a murmur of love:
Night and Ocean loved one another, and hope
Seemed to speak better of God than on a good day.
Sailors slept, rocked by nature,

Like children on their mother's breast;
Venus, on the horizon, shined powerful and pure;
One barely heard in the vast murmur
The silent sound of eternal weeping.
– In the face of Night with its sublime depths,
Don't you feel then, O mortals, – O victims, –
Exhilarations when looking at the Sky?

Lasciate Ogni Speranza...[12]

*Now is the time to bury all songs, good and bad.
Go find me a large casket, make sure it is large like the
great tower of Heidelberg, and bring me twelve giants to
carry it and throw it into the sea.*

– For so large a casket, a large grave is needed.

– Do you know why it will be so large and so heavy?

*– I will deposit into it, at the same time, both my love and
my sufferings.*

— Heinrich Heine

At the hour when the leaden-eyed Orgy lifts
Its fatal hand to smash its drinking cup against the
         wall,
I stopped forgetting, amidst the impure tumult,
     She who sleeps, tranquil and pure.

Farewell, you whom my voice will never awaken
         again!
Into the grave, I saw my childhood follow you...

[12]*Lasciate Ogni Speranza:* Italian for "Let go of all hope."

For really great hearts, great sorrow lived through,
    Encourages living.

Far from me that crowd with its confused
        stammering!
My soul is like the rocks whose lofty peaks,
Seeing the waves escape, lean their empty caves
    O'er their own abysses.

Farewell then, days of childhood, O beautiful days
        filled with hope!
Muse, don't you know any immortal songs?
Come! The eagle, in order to fly, need only see
    The immensity before its wings!

Song of Calvary

Song the First

Lama Sabachthani[13]

> *Ecce civitas Santi facta est deserta; Sion deserta facta est. –*
> *Jerusalem desolata est: domus sanctificationis tuae et*
> *gloriae tuae, ubi laudaverunt te patres nostri![14]*

> – Psalms.

I

It was Venus Day. The Asian proconsuls
Had, in the name of the Gods, ordered pleasure;
And in Jerusalem, the insouciant athlete,
Following his fancy, exhausted himself in leisure.
The Ancients inhaled ardent sensual delights
In the warm atriums where Bacchantes danced;
Disks crossed through space during contests;
And myrtles quaked in the victors' fists.

– Slaves on that day were allowed to conceal,

---

[13]*Lama sabachthani*: Matthew 27:45. The full text, in Greek, is
"Eli, eli, lama sabachthani" which means "My God, My God, why
hast thou forsaken me."

[14]Isaiah 64:10-11.

Under the Roman toga, their irons and misfortunes. –
Joyful little children gamboled on the plain,
Casting a mocking smile at their pedagogues.
At the bottom of fresh gullies, stretched out on the
     moss,
Rhetor disciples listened gravely
To the deep, sonorous voice of old sages;
On the grass, a little farther away, it was entirely
     different:
Venus took her Bacchus for a constant playmate.
On the peaceful mountains of Gilboa and Golgotha,
Suspended above the open country, flocks pastured.
On a somber butte, near Golgotha,
Alone, between two gibbets, a cross stood.

It was Venus Day! Far from Jewish customs,
Pensive vestal virgins, white in their peplums,
Rested their elbows on the altar, captive in their
     temples.
Their goddess was still cold in her marble.
On a silver tripod in the nocturnal hall,
The solitary flame flashed in the urn, all
    A glow, like a reflection of their loves.

And the sun tinged the sycamore woods gold;
A thousand zephyrs ran though the sonorous leaves;
Old wines poured from amphoras into impluviums;
Heaven's purity colored the horizon blue;
Reapers slept in bed beside their sickles,
Young men laughed with young women
    Under Sion's olive trees.

And nailed to his Cross, he examined the earth...

Pensive, he contemplated life and light;
Beneath him, on a rock, his mother wept;
The moss shone, birds warbled.
Bent over unfathomable and superb nature,
He watched while under the palms, amidst the
        flowers,
  The children played in the grass.

And all were happy! all, even the slaves.
He lifted towards death two gorgeous, blue, and
        serious eyes.
The robbers struggled, shaking their shackles:
The muted hour passed silently into infinity;
Then, bowing his head onto his chest
He cried, with a divine and expiring voice:
  "Eli! Lama Sabachthani!"

II

Suddenly, a wave of darkness fell, obliterating the
        daylight.
Three gibbets, trembling under their doleful weights,
Cracked in the shadow by the wind. Over his vacant
        expressions,
Agony extended its bloody hands;
On the hill, where the three crosses were planted,
Light cast shadows with silver tints onto
  The three pallid crucified men!

From broken sepulchers rose strange cries;
Fleet lightning flashed, swords of archangels;
The blood-reddened tree was wet with sweat;
And night extinguished the celestial vault's golden

    fires,
And heaven extended profoundly like doubt.
And the stars vacillated, hesitating in route;
    Everything was scandal and terror!

Oh! What did he mean by those unknown words
Cried from the height of suffering, – Then, the
      man with a lance
Arrived: but Christ was inanimate now.
Carrying unto death the meaning of his mystery,
The Son of Man had left earth behind.
– And as for us, it was quite finished on Calvary,
    Lord! All was consummated.

It is said that then, breaking the vault of clouds,
An expanse of sky opened up with radiant splendors.
– Invisible to human beings filled with obscurities,
God shone deep down onto his radiant work.
The Universe froze in awful expectation,
And night itself, seized with Terror,
    Recoiled before the brightness.

On the azure spheres ablaze with light,
Seraphim leant over, engulfed in ecstasy,
And illuminated the altars with their loving souls:
And their appearance appeased the angels of
      destruction;
And the somber accords of their divine lyres
Accompanied the name of the thorn-crowned man
    In their immortal hymns.

III

– O Tenebrae! – Your spheres, thus suspended
Over the abyss, had they not descended in answer to
        that cry?
And had they not pummeled creation with lightning,
Had they not darkened the Earth in the middle of your
        Expanses?
Meanwhile, in the brightness of their destruction,
Cain's children would have read your true name,
Jehovah! – the man, at least, in that late hour
Would have known the secret of his own dust!
From the fatal instant of his first sigh,
What he is doing here below? – Forgetting and
        suffering! –
Is this life? To ignore the reason for one's living,
And, without knowing why, chased from the void,
Marched into exile, alone, sad, abandoned,
Where his archangel's pride, forever degraded,
Is pulled down by the weight of his melancholy?!
Where, because he was born, dispersed by chance
Into a corner of earth called the fatherland,
He must, – obscure phantom of crime and madness, –
Change consciousness while changing the past!
He must, without knowing whether he prays or
        blasphemes,
Kindle in himself, forever and ever,
The flame of a *Maybe*, both uncertain and supreme?...
At that last hour of death, worn down by abandon,
If he turns towards you, calm God of pardon,
Is it because he believes? – A last word of Doubt
Is the voice that murmurs in his ear: "Listen!
He was *perhaps* a God: he is *perhaps* a Savior..."

– For we have Doubt buried in our heart.
Those days are gone when Roman strength
Dispatched sovereign reason to the pyre
By the will of mighty warriors with an all-powerful
        Sword,
Who tinged their blazons in a human purple
And who knew how to sign their names – but only in
        blood!
– The Cross blinded them with its profound light
And, failing to enlighten them, they burned worlds of
        them!
But many more of the still more fastidious so-called
        beings,
Remain among us, are ours... – our great savants!
Alone, on our ruins, like orfrays,[15]
Choosing scattered bones for milestones,
They have dissected God, those funereal old men!
And, counting and sounding and recounting the
        wounds,
Their debased scalpels are nothing but knives!
– What's the point of judging them? Who knows
        what's at the bottom of things?
Everyone marches down the path to a common end
Where are the sole causes of the evil that governs
        us?
A small part of the truth – taken for the whole truth!
Look at our feet, without overemphasizing!
Divine belief has trembled on its bases.
Isn't it gold that sounds all its triumphant knells?
One sells a young girl to a sickly old man
And, in a vile gambling den, the fathers of families
Gamble away, under everyone's eyes, their children's

---

[15]orfrays: from French *orfrais,* a variant of osprey.

      bread!
Look! The young are keeling over before their time!
Pleasure without grandeur! Orgy with a straight face,
With the people below who devour their fury!
A pale whirlwind of blasé egoists!...
– No one reads anymore, they yawn; and they tell
        you, "Pass."
Unbridled adultery, prodigious vampire!
No one knowing really, anymore, what they wanted
        to say;
Words don't express a thing, laws make people laugh
Sadly. And the hatred! and the abuse! forever!...
– Never has man suffered as in our days... –
And all the unfortunate folk, whose morose contempt,
Because it laughs at everything, believes it knows
        something,
Call this nightmare a reality!
They have mocked, I believe, holy probity;
This century is a pig that lets its rutting muffle slaver
On the muck it sucks up along the way!
Your mysterious Cyrenian man,[16]
On grim Golgotha, will not come back, doubtless,
To help carry the cross of their destiny
For the outstretched arms of Cain's children!
This sketch is lugubrious, grim, and veridical!
– It does not get any gloomier than this before
        Eternity:
They jeer!... and, rhetors full of metaphysics,
If that's the end result, sure! It is magnificent!...
– But they are discontented with living, in all
        honesty!

---

[16]Cyrenian: Simon the Cyrene, who was recorded as having helped the Christ carry his cross.

The thinker, today, admits of no belief system:
The thinker today believes only what he can feel.
His deep despair dictates his blasphemy,
And in a God, made man, he sees only a martyr!
– Lord, we contemplate that single aureole
On your face crowned with love and contempt:
Come back then and save us! Your celestial word,
A prey to the agony where all hope escapes,
When you died for us, O Lord, you promised.
Our soul is dazzled by your divine story.
But, seeing the winding sheet on the cross, Jesus,
Alas! human pride wants to understand in order to
            believe:
And we admire you too much to be convinced.
One feels, dreaming of it, the shiver of the abyss.
And we have concluded, all ready to adore you:
If God came, he would be called Jesus;
Before his devotion, to doubt it would be... a crime!...
Let's bow down then, and try to pray!

Song the Second

Evohe Bacchus[17]

*Peccavimus, et facti sumus tanquam immundus nos, et
cecidimus quasi folium universi, et iniquitates nostrae,
quasi ventus, abstulerunt nos! – Abscundisti faciem tuam a*

---

[17]Original footnote: In the 787th year of Rome, on the 8th day of
the calends of April: Rubellius Geminus and Fusius Geminus
being consuls: [it is] a holiday. – Tiberius is 19 years, ten months,
and twenty days old. J.C. is thirty-two and a half.

nobis, et allisisti nos in manu iniquitatis nostrae![18]

– Psalms

I

Under the thick cedars, near the river, at a certain
      hour,
Whilst a poor mother wept at the Christ's feet,
In the marble villa with its numerous stairs
Bathing their white feet in amorous waves,
The young patricians, with open tunics
Made of purple and gold, covered in diamonds,
Cup in hand, eyes exhausted by languors,
Reclining on tricliniums and crowned with flowers,
– They celebrated you, Venus, Queen of Saturnalias,
Goddess of the night! –

II

      – Pallid courtesans
Poured Massico wine for them, with its ardent
      aromas. –
Those women of Italy! They were so beautiful;
And, as they leapt up, their rebellious chests
Exposed their naked breasts outside the white veils!
Their black hair, luxuriant and somber mantles,
Bedecked by countless pearls and amber beads,
Covered their alabaster arms and their charmed
      lovers
With the voluptuous folds of their scented waves.
How well they pivoted on their lascivious hips!
Under fervid kisses their convulsive lips,

---

[18]*Peccavimus... nostrae*: From the *Rorate Caeli*, or Isaiah 64:5-7.

Coral corollas, softly convulsed
Into a moist smile, a protracted quivering...
The diffuse sounds of theorbos, lutes, and mandores
Fell onto the sonorous tiles, thoroughly shivering:
And sometimes the night's harmonious blasts
Touched their golden chords as they returned to
   heaven.
African slaves, ambrosia cupbearers,
Carried the silver amphora on their black heads;
Cups were emptied in silence, at present,
In order to revive the superb orgy's passion.
– Venus mocked Jesus as he expired on the Cross.
The clepsydra flowed and told the ninth hour...
Then, in the back gardens of the residence
Torches flamed. – On the waters, near the sacred
   wood,
Chords and voices were heard.

III

Hymn to Venus

Song of Slaves

1

O Venus with the charming face!
From the height of her savage throne
When Phoebus colors the shore

On the starry orb of the night,
The fishers of coral often see your image
Which bathes in silence, and then, like a cloud,
        Vanishes!...

2

It is the pale hour of mysteries...
The cliffs are solitary...
Rocking on the bitter waves
Is the shadow of your graceful body:
O Venus, evening flower!... On the light algae
Rest the rays of your soft lights
        From seventh heaven.

3

O beautiful child of wet waves,
To you my Numidian mares,
My bow, my casque, and my chlamydes,
To you my heart, and to you my days;
To you my javelins and my splendid palaces,
And my white mistress and my fleet arrows
        And my loves.

IV

In the Gardens

Scene One

LYNCEUS, a fifteen-year-old child; SEMPRONIA, a courtesan: she is twenty-six years old. They are walking under the lofty branches of the cedars. Statues. The last couplet of the slaves' Hymn to Venus dies down in the distance.

LYNCEUS
They sing well, what do you say?

SEMPRONIA
                                        Not bad, I think,
For slaves...

LYNCEUS
Smiling.
So be it, as long as you like it...
Me, however, I rather like the air of that romance
Which the evening bird sings, amidst the silence,
        Among the plane trees of the forest...
And you?

SEMPRONIA
                Perhaps!... Child, look how soft the
Verdure is under our feet, how pure the night is!
In the trireme, far away, the rowers are sleeping...
Everything is quiet!

LYNCEUS
                        Love alone is still awake in our
        hearts!

SEMPRONIA
Immortal gods! The night, strewn with stars,
Surrounds the universe with an embalmed embrace...
Oh! be my universe; and I will be your night!

She fastens, languidly, her arms around
Lynceus's neck.

LYNCEUS

O my Sempronia!

SEMPRONIA

Come! Venus leads us!...
Venus shines through the tenebrous branches...
Child! I am happy among the happiest...
So much so that I suffer.

LYNCEUS

Today, never having
Seen you before, O prodigy! It seems to me however
That I know you already...

They walk for a while without speaking.

SEMPRONIA
Raising her head.

The dark thunderstorms
No longer rumble... The moon casts a silver light o'er
the clouds... – O flowers!... One must love! Lynceus,
love me then... – O gorgeous night!

LYNCEUS

It is charming,

just like you!

They walk off.

In the Villa

The triclinium. A hall with divers styles of architecture, in the Roman fashion. Statues of Asiatic gods. It is a pleasure house designed to receive consuls. The young people from Rome, traveling in Asia, were received there with their retinue. Men and women are reclining on opulent litters made from the hides of savage beasts. They speak amongst themselves, while waiting for their drunkenness to increase in order to celebrate the Augustan festival. Etruscan lamps are suspended from the ceilings, in the recesses of the colonnades. Small iron chains support immense purple-black, thrice-dyed Oriental drapes. Between the pillars, trophies taken from Barbarians shine. At the very back is the altar consecrated to Venus-Astarte and to Lyaeus-Bacchus.

Black slaves, with gold rings on their feet and hands, and dressed in antique fabrics, walk about silent and grave. The women burn incense.

The guards watch from the villa's steps.

Scene Two

The Men: THE POET CELSUS, SEXTUS LUCIUS MARCELLUS, SEPTIMUS MARCIUS CASCA, SEXTUS SCIPIO, THE FREED SLAVE DAVUS, A CYNIC PHILOSOPHER. *The Women*: LUCILIA, FULVIA, BATHYLLE, NEREA, MATELLA, CYNTHIA. And also THE SLAVES.

The guests no longer speak, and they drink in silence, intertwined. – The Cynic philosopher observes them, leaning his back against a column.

SEXTUS LUCIUS MARCELLUS
Rising.

Magdalena?

FULVIA
It's true! What has happened to her?
For nearly two months now nobody has seen her.
She becomes vestal.

BATHYLLE
In fact... it's a means to
Stifle her boredom.

THE FREED SLAVE DAVUS
To Metella.
She sure danced well,
That girl!

METELLA
Yes.

SEXTUS SCIPIO
Who can keep her from her
fate?

BATHYLLE
What good is that: perhaps she is dead.

SEXTUS LUCIUS MARCELLUS
I miss her limid eyes and her white arms,
And above all her gracious and strong spirit.
– That was under the praetor Pontius, in Rome, on the
Ides
Of March; At that time I was in the Senate. Subsidies
From the Northern militias redounded to me. I took
One thousand sesterces in gold, and I offered them to
her.

Sejanus, that individual with the avid phrases,
Wanted her as much as I did. Might the Eumenides
Strangle her, if he's the one she has gone off with,
        and may Charon
Refuse her obolus at the banks of Acheron!
She cost me little; she had a nice soul.
To be sure, I almost loved her.

NEREA
                        Amazing lunacy!
And how did all that finish?

SEXTUS LUCIUS MARCELLUS
                        As all things do... One
knows not how. – Hmm! By boredom, by disgust
Of me. – I'm thirsty!

A slave refills his cup.

                        This Ponce has some sublime
wine!... It's proof he has taste! The rascal has my
        esteem.

He drinks. – Lucilia speaks to him in a low voice.

SEXTUS LUCIUS MARCELLUS
To Lucilia.
By Venus! not yet. One must rest now.

Lucilia distances herself. – He continues drinking.

CYNTHIA
Near the suspended balconies, addressing Celsus.

The evening wind is warm and gentle like a kiss.

THE POET CELSUS

Cynthia, listen to me!... Your mouth which murmurs
Is like an open pomegranate: is it ripe yet?...
Let me see it!

They kiss.

THE CYNIC PHILOSOPHER

Passing near them, smiling.

These are, I believe, very tender
fruits... They are often eaten: between meals even.

He distances himself. – Silence.

CYNTHIA

Some time later.

Lie down at my feet!

THE POET CELSUS

Good! Why?

CYNTHIA

I beg you,
Give me your hair to mess up a bit!... I'm bored.

They look at each other laughing.

SEPTIMUS MARCIUS CASCA

He takes a piece of papyrus in hand and draws on it.

Who was talking about Sejanus?

SEXTUS LUCIUS MARCELLUS
Rising.
Me.

SEPTIMUS MARCIUS CASCA
I'm drawing his
portrait:
Admire!
He passes his drawing around.

LUCILIA
That hunchback?

NEREA
Vulcan would be less ugly!

SEPTIMUS MARCIUS CASCA
He's going to be married; it's a wedding gift.
But for a talent of gold, I'd reduce the hump.

Laughter by the Cynic philosopher.

FULVIA
Smiling
If he gets wind of that, to start with he'll dispatch
His sword-carrying lictor after you...

SEPTIMUS MARCIUS CASCA
Lifting his cup.
Ah! will he have
me slayed?
Infernal gods, I drink to you! – Pour, vestal. –
It's all empty. –

Silence.

ECHO IN THE NIGHT
– Empty!... –

THE CYNIC PHILOSOPHER
To himself, sadly.
              The frightening death rattle!...
Are those the living there?

He looks them over, and remains pensive.

SEPTIMUS MARCIUS CASCA
              By Pluto! my friend,
I will be dead tomorrow; today I must drink!...

SEXTUS SCIPIO
His eyes fixed on the trophies.
Oh! to a master... a Sejanus! – May our morose heads
From this moment forward be crowned with nothing
but roses!... – What do they do, our forebears, on their
dismal sojourns?

THE CYNIC PHILOSOPHER
They gaze!...

SEPTIMUS MARCIUS CASCA
You think?

To the slave.

              Then, keep pouring!

Bursts of laughter.

SEXTUS LUCIUS MARCELLUS
Now, I feel better.

He looks around, yawning.

– If I had a wife?
– Is there anything left?

THE POET CELSUS
Let's go, a soulless body
For M. Marcellus!

Scene Three

SAME PEOPLE
SEMPRONIA re-enters leaning on LYNCEUS's arm.

SEMPRONIA
Hearing the last words, to Marcellus/
Hey Knight! Do you want a
piece?

SEXTUS LUCIUS MARCELLUS
Gladly!

LYNCEUS
Staggering.
Is it true?... Did I hear that correctly?...

SEMPRONIA
Fine! You will have me again when your desire
  returns!

She goes off with Sextus Lucius Marcellus.

LYNCEUS
In a low voice.
Great Gods! Is it possible?

He lays his hand on his poignard.

THE POET CELSUS
Breaking out in laughter behind him.
                        Child! But that's life!

*He presents a cup to him. – Lynceus refuses it with a
gesture, and leaves the room slowly.*

SEXTUS LUCIUS MARCELLUS
Pointing out Lynceus with his finger, to Sempronia.
Does he displease you that young man?

SEMPRONIA
Naturally.

                                        Him?...

No.

*She smiles at him with a surprised expression;
they sit.*

After a few moments, the inebriation has made their expressions
shine. The slaves have removed their golden rings and recline on
the steps of the altar consecrated to Bacchus. One slave girl turns

over the hourglass: the torches burn behind the drapes. A strange
music, composed of citherns, tambours, cymbals, and Phrygian
flutes, resonates suddenly; Metella gets up, brandishing a
panther skin, exalted and half-naked.

METELLA
Sing us the song of Bacchus, Scipion!

Everyone gets up and circles round the altar. The last Scipion
throws at the foot of the statue his crown of roses and lotus
leaves, and sings with a vibrant voice. Outside, only night and
silence.

SEXTUS SCIPIO
Raising his cup.

1st couplet.
Death sharpens his somber scythe,
Romans get drunk in the shade...
The night has its countless scents!
The Night has enchanted eyes:
    – Evohë Bacchë!
Evohë! This thirst devours us!
Naked Bacchante, oh! Strike again
The tympanum with a loud blow
With your bloody thyrsi!
    – Bacchus, ëvohë!

EVERYONE
At full voice.
– Evohë Bacchus

SEXTUS SCIPIO

2nd couplet.

God of Satyrs and Fauns;
God of brilliant yellow vine branches;
You, who know how to chase from thrones
The care of realities:
    – Evohë Bacchë!
Come, to the solitary cenacle,
Consoling God of the earth,
Pour your salutary liquor
With mysterious gaieties!
    – Bacchus, ëvohë!

EVERYONE
– Evohë Bacchus!

SEXTUS SCIPIO

3rd couplet.

Come! Your vagabond priestesses
Vacate the old-world woods...
Alone, we sing to deep nights,
Tired of our heavy majesties:
    – Evohë Bacchë!
Grant forgetfulness, God of Inebriation!
In mortal goddesses' arms
Burn our faces with your caresses
And our hearts with your sensual pleasures:
    – Bacchus, ëvohë!

EVERYONE
With the terrible cries of joy.
– Evohë Bacchus!

Here, diverse scenes of debauchery, in the formidable and antique fashion.

V

Stanzas

1

Sing! sing, glittering and pale Romans!
Roll your withered bodies in the thick of Saturnalias!
It is the law! Rejoice, O you preferred by fate!
He who laughs this evening, tomorrow shivers and
   weeps!
Attila, sinister reaper, waits for the hour
When the golden ears of wheat that the West wind
   touches
  Are ripe for the North wind!

2

Up! To arms, Gauls! O Sicambrian slaves!
The awakened people will break their fetters...
The world is a volcano and you are the lava!...
March! Rome is perhaps still a memory.
May the sword strike and rumble on your bucklers,
Knell of the past, sounding the world's ruin!...
  Scourge, you are the future!

3

They have become old, their eagles useless!
They go to tear themselves apart in their civil wars...
What can they say to victorious songs?

– Ah! the childish old men who devour at feasts,
For several happy days, centuries of conquests,
Must find the rusted casques of their ancestors
    Quite heavy at present on their heads.

4

What do they have left of their ancestors and their
      proud courage?
Their thirst for blood: that's their cowardly
      heritage!...
And soon the hour will arrive when savage lions
Will wait crouching, with fire in their eyes, for
Those great banner bearers of the Church
      Triumphant,
Martyrs that will be torn apart in the arena
    To relieve the Caesars' boredom!

VI

A Clearing in the Sacred Woods

Scene Four

LYNCEUS is alone. He comes and sits down by the river. The nightingale sings under the leaves. After several moments of reflection and struggles, the young man removes his tunic. His great blond hair falls over his shoulders. He speaks to himself in a half-voice.

I will never see you again, O Roman countrysides...

The shepherds I loved will forget me on your plains.
And you alone, O Diana, star dear to the deceased,
Will know that I'm dead in the distant waves,
On a night of love, flowers, and perfumes!

He throws himself into the river. Suddenly the voice of
Sempronia rises above the sounds of a lute. She repeats the tune
of the song sung by the fishermen to Venus. The river rolls its
green waves and the nightingale resumes its interrupted tune.

SEMPRONIA
In the villa.

. . . .
O Venus, evening flower!... Pose the rays of your
        soft lights
From seventh heaven on the light algae.

VII

Where, then, was the Magdalena?
Venus' white daughter
With the sensual breath?
Why did she no longer return?
They would have wanted to see her shiver
Again, under their sonorous kisses,
Her charming body's alabaster.
But, doubtless, in the residence,
She was sleeping, at this hour,
In her lover's arms.

Song the Third

Sancta Magdalena

*Vide, Domine, afflictionem populi tui, et
mitte quem missurus es. – Emitte Agnum
dominatorem terrae; de petra deserti, ad
montem filiae Sion, ut auferat, ipse, jugum
captivitatus nostrae!*[19]

   – Psalms

1

It was Golgotha! The wind, like a moan,
Surged. Calvary was bathed in blood...
Gloomy terrors, alas! At the foot of the holy Cross,
Something like a cadaver was lying:
There was a human shade, immobile, stretched out,
A woman's form; and, like a statue,
She stayed like that silently.
The buriers were supposed to arrive, nevertheless!...

Covered in darkness, Jerusalem slept;
The grass extended, in the distance, its green
      lividness.
The crown of thorns, as well as rays of light,
On the head of the Christ, with sepulchral pallor,
Shined. At times, in the sky shred into furrows,
Mute claps of thunder rolled like death rattles;
White flashes of lightning burst out like visions.

---

[19]*Vide, Domine*...: from the *Rorate Cæli* Mass.

2

Choir of Definite Spirits

"O you whom pleasure calls,
O young woman with blonde hair,
Since the night makes you so beautiful,
Since love is in your eyes,
What are you doing near those slaves?
Tears make grave stigmata!
You will wear out your smooth traits...
And the time to live is limited.
Listen to their distant songs of drunkenness...
What are you doing, beautiful enchantress?
Lucius asks his mistress;
Love asks beauty!
Recall, recall the flowers of your years,
The devouring perfumes of your pleasure bed,
        Of your untied waistbands
Falling onto the cothurnus with its molded shapes
        As soon as desire approaches!"

3

The storm howls mournful;
The moon, with its horn,
Like that of a worn floweret,
A vermillion diadem.
The infernal hordes
Of spectral sibyls
Leave their sleep
And, banging their cymbals,
Dance in the pale shimmers

Of the sun's sister.

Choir of Sibyls

"Glory, love, hope, faith, youth,
Religions, crimes, remorses...
Sister, everything leaves us in old age
    And death.
On my large baton, mount thy crupper!
He's a beautiful God, your lover is!...
The earthworm laughs and sups
    Tranquilly."

The earth vacillated under their unbridled waltz.
A chasm, upon each step, opened under their feet:
The phantoms soon disappeared... – Smoke!
– The Cross alone remained. – All was thick clouds;
    It was Doubt that passed.

4

Thus, ever since the time that the ruin encumbers,
Neither the terrible humiliation of the red coat,
Nor, at night, their countless smiles,
Nor the painful tapping of the hammer,
Nor the potter's field, that infamous tomb,
Nor the scepter of opprobrium in your bound hands,
Nor even, in your face, the black finger of
    disapproval,
Nothing, but nothing, on the tree where you hanged,
Could uproot your faith which lasts for years,
    O Crucified Man of Golgotha!

Yes, the impure punishment; the slave's funereal
Apparatuses: a gibbet erected in the darkness;
The humble glory of a God shone all around him.
Not a single ray was lacking at his sovereign death:
Cross, not even your nails; Jew, not even your hatred;
    Woman, not even your love!

5

– Redeemer! we too have our Calvaries!
And, while we might forget them, your heaven may
      not.
– And our loves, wept over or betrayed, here on earth!
And our pride deflated by bitter humiliations!
Alas! Emmanuel! but your memories alone
Would suffice to trouble the azure of lofty spheres...
And we have all abandoned the faith of our fathers
    At the bottom of their shrouds' folds!
Oh! we have, however, when Joy or Grief
Made our days languid with their heavy hands,
Cried: "Lord! Lord!" to the impassive stars
Which responded: "Maybe!" but which continued to
      shine!
Often, young still, during nights of delirium,
Hoping for something holy from Love,
We looked for God in a smile...
    But the smile faded.
Often kneeling before the last remnants
Of those whose appearance and voice we loved,
Yes, we have looked for celestial visions
From this God, simultaneously hoped for and
      feared!...
Nothing! – Often, proud, joining our hot hands

together
Before the immensity of shimmering seas,
When dawn revealed its immortal mirage
In the fields of light darkened by the clouds,
We said: "Lord, are those your works there?"
     But all remained silent under heaven;
No voice spoke. When in tempests,
Or on happy days, when inclining our heads,
We said: "Creator of silent lights
Where are you now, Lord, you who hide thus?"
No seas nor flowers nor a profound dawn,
Nor the star of heaven, nor this world's virgin,
Nor the cross on a tombstone, nothing responds:
     "Here!"

Man has made up his mind, moreover: he laughs and
          eats;
He sings, kills, drinks. As for God, let him fend for
          himself!
What is the reason for his condition! – Boredom!
Boredom is the iron tunic that oppresses him today!
He summed up everything with this one word:
     "Phenomenon!"
A sad word muttered by human ignorance
Under the ragged coat of science. Ah! the forbidden
          tree
Has given the juice of its old twisted fruit alright!
The living have drained the cup of drunkenness:
On reawakening, sadness follows after disgust.
The malediction of precocious old women
Makes young men bend over their withered loins.
O old world! In the shadows where your brave are
          buried,

Those august majesties who took up your crimes,
Those virtues, that honor, with its strict maxims,
Words engraved at the heart of your sublime
              centuries,
Time, that gravedigger, it has, like them, cut them
              down.
O martyrs! who among us believes in your suffering?
Were you not joyous in your torment?
The angel of hope stood beside you!
It smiled with love on your last moments!
You felt its white wings flutter in your face
And its divine kisses stifled your sobs;
And death, while chilling your pure and faithful heart
Changed your executioners' cries into melodious
              concerts.
Death was there, watching your life lean over
In gusts of grief, like a faded flower,
To transport it, serene and triumphant, to God.
Your soul was elected before you were born...
You saw nothing in the sky but the blue!
One would like, with you, to change destiny:
And inspired and sobbing priests would like, we too,
To expire like you, while believing like you!

6

You know what you do, O woman who weeps!
Your thought was lofty in your wide demesnes,
Long ago! – even old men appreciated your mind.
You know all the delirium that dawn gives birth to,
And all the smiles that day illuminates,
        O you who weep in the night!

Didn't you live rich, beautiful, intoxicated,
Free bird, barely alighting on a country,
Making the tribunes' heads bow to your knees,
Until you yourself, insouciant and proud,
Spread over your feet both love and prayer
     With the incense of your perfumes?

It is you then whom one must ask whether joy
Is hidden in love! The ardent love that makes
Fervent breasts buckle under young kisses;
Or from cups of gold, crowned with roses,
That one drinks whilst singing in the morning of life,
     In an age when everyone speaks of God.

In an age when one floats down rivers in baskets
In the South!... there, where, on its wings
The warm Asian wind wafts through banana trees
The scents of beaches, the farewells of cherished
          flowers,
The gentle splashing sounds of waves, reveries,
     And the seafarers' song.

Or if true happiness hides in tears,
Close to crosses in the desert of nocturnal alarms,
Under the bite of the cilice embracing a wasted
          body,
If Faith can gush from the sorrow that denies,
As when, to the weary traveler, a blessed spring
     Surges from the rock that has wounded him.

Are you looking for forgiveness, hope, courage,
In the celestial blood that bathes your visage?
And the superhuman love that your heart has

    suffered,
Does it make you scorn life's loves?
And should we disdain everything that invites us
    To die in the Desert?

No: but at the moment when he was leaving nature,
When his mother lay expressionless, without a sound,
Seeing you there among the frightened executioners,
Perhaps he said something to you, on account
Of your divine love! a secret... something...
    One last word, to you.

For after seeing you, O pale female enthusiast,
Under the frightful trees devastated by autumn,
Drunk on heaven, lying down, a half-naked body,
On the sacred leaves, alone, with a finger, dreaming,
You indicated in the dark some thing between the
        lines,
    Something that no one understood!...

7

And now, farewell! silent vestiges
That watch over an austere beauty in the dust!
Farewell then, ancient world where so many great
        wonders
Have signaled the end of your great city!
– Ah! you immolated them, those Christians, at your
        festivals!
The fiery words of your gloomy prophets,
In bygone times, had really predicted it for you!
The blow of the axe, the chopping off heads,
Made your Gods tumble away into the eternal night!

Their charming ghosts don't love your marble
   anymore!...
O celestial Apollo! O Bacchus, god of kings!
And you, Venus' son who, looking into your quiver
For arrows, pursued through the great woods
Those nymphs who fled you, with wet feet, under
   the trees!
Let's go! It's quite finished now. Your altar's flowers
Crown your tombs, O young immortals!

But if we stay here on earth, old world, alone,
To drag our disinherited steps into oblivion;
If we and our century, children of a dark mystery,
March on your dust, on the bones of your weary;
If our angered skies, in our profound nights,
Are nothing but the winding sheets of your divinities,
If we no longer love anything, not even our young,
If our hearts are filled with pointless sadnesses,
If nothing for us of neither kings nor Gods remains,
Let us at least keep, like a last flame, the Cross!

Ballade[20]

One has not forgotten the provocations of certain pages in the English press. In addition to those things of the journals, phrases that have been put forward in the form of toasts at our neighbors' banquets, in the following vein: "Their tricolor flag, emblem of tyranny, is covered with crimes and murders. – I drink to its judgment at the tribunal of universal equity, and to its near abolition." Then, on the subject of Saint-Helena, a man said: "An example for the oppressors of liberty." – Pretty bouquet of realism! There's nothing like the flowery banks of the Thames to inspire such gracious politico-splenetic outbursts. – It merited a smile at best; however, more or less analogous words have so many times been pronounced in our presence that the author, succumbing to a feeling of natural indignation, wanted to respond to them on everyone's behalf.

I

O people!.. since when has France's oriflamme,
Which flew for eight hundred years at the end of a
    lance,
Had to be accountable for what goes on here, by
    chance?
Who dares then to run down its ancient memory?
The times judge kings, man judges history...
    A God alone judges the standard. –

The flag of a country is the country itself;
Ours is the shroud and the emblem of heroes,
The restraint of foreigners and the honor of soldiers;
It is our dead ancestors who watch, in the shadows;

---

[20]Ballade: This poem is a first attempt of what later became the abbreviated poem entitled "A Manner of Imitating M. De Pompignan."

It is our standing altar, freed from a somber yoke,
  It is our heart finally that beats!

From time immemorial, whenever that might be,
   under its beloved colors,
It made honor wave at our armies' vanguard;
It could be vanquished, sometimes; – never faded. –
And when someone comes again to outrage its
  valiance,
Our old standard unfurls in silence
  And signals the cannons to respond for it. –

The veritable name that is borne, in Life, by
Napoléon, Bourbon, Valois..., it is "The Fatherland."
What does a great country care for the color of its
  flag?
– Eagle or golden *fleur-de-lys*, that's a question for
  the times:
Those enemy heroes, brothers by their courage,
  God reunites them in the grave.

II

– Joan of Arc's Englishmen! – you've lost your
   memory.
By what right durst you tarnish the sacred history
Of the flag before which you've all trembled?
Englishmen, you know, these kinds of things are
   cowardly. –
Look past the noble folds to find the marks within.
  You'll find only holes. –

Holes, those are the bloody eyes of the tricolor eagle:

From atop their poles, they fix their warm eyes still
On the martyred Emperor; and eagles see keenly. –
Oh! be careful not to trouble the silence:
In our days, life is short for the sons of France,
    – But lightning strikes at the speed of light. –

As he reposes at last on the shores of the Seine,
– Keep down, jailers of St. Helena,[21]
Your belated courage, – don't wake him.
Don't wake him in his great stone bed!
France is sometimes quite near to England...
    Englishmen, Englishmen, speak softer. –

III

Dream then! If he had left suddenly... – Beautiful
        dream! –
To consult with pensive Death: "Wait for me to rise:
I will return. Hold on, watch over my child here."
And at the sound of his boots on livid tiles,
The mutilated remnants of his old invalids
Went to prick up their ears, and look at him!

In the middle of the night, with his proud smile,
If he appeared, arms crossed, to say to them:
"Up, soldiers, it's me." Then, how their green
        cannons,
In the shadows, illuminated by a terrifying joy,
Began blasting, belching their formidable salvoes,
Their sounds completely congested by rust, and alone
        capable

---

[21]As he reposes... St. Helena: The reference is to Napoléon Bonaparte.

Of shaking the thunderous echos of the universe!

IV

"It's me! Tambours! bugles! But my glorious eagle,
Would it have seen close up the other black eagle
While I was already sleeping? – As you can see,
It appears to have grown at least after one victory!...
You can tell me all about it, *en route*. –
As for you, my executioners, wait: – Someone should
        toll
The bell of England! – And may it rumble and
        resound
As far as Notre-Dame! – Enough lived! – I wish that
        now
The tocsin announced to the world that the Avenger
Is at hand. – Attack! – You, inflamed battle,
Let your reddened cannonballs whistle through the
        smoke!
Let the trench burst in a deluge of fire!
– O soldiers! if night falls, would that our sublime
        eagle
Might perch atop my head and act as a torch for you:
Let's go, living cyclone, scale the chasm
That your ancestors would have straddled!"

V

– People! – it would be only a blow to the head, in
        summary:
– If he did it, however, all of a sudden, the old man
Of bronze? – If he rose up from the bottom of his
        coffin, as

Recently from Elba Island? – Ah! it's just that, you
      see,
He needs to rest a bit. – Besides, always vanquishing!
That wears a man down. – And, in order to convince
      you,
See how weary he is! – He's sleeping quite nicely
      now, no? –
Then, it's because he suffered like a martyr
In respect to his size, impossible to tell you!
Come on... think about it... there was a rock...
One slept there at gunpoint, and then, it was too dear
The water he drank... He always saw the shoulders
Of Englishmen, – as in combat, – they laughed at
      him, the rogues.
Sometimes he exited, under the watchful eyes of
      prison guards,
To gaze at the sea with its blue waves roaring beneath
      his feet...

It was horrible. – In the end, it's only England
That in that situation there makes you its prisoner! ...
Isn't that right now, that it should be quiet?
And no longer extol to us, in its mad furor,
A jailor's opprobrium before a French Emperor?

VI

But... not to fear! – It's only a dream...
Englishmen... here comes the dawn, – he's escaped. –
Next to an executioner stands a sword,
One must wait until he has it. –
Wait then too, you, poet!
Alas! in spite of this festive sky,

A bloody future unsettles you
And the present makes you weep:
It's that, you see, your country founders,
Its young people lack youthfulness,
You must understand in your sadness
What you have just expressed. –

VII

Recall, however, the Crimean eagles,
And then the hero Lourmel;[22] conscripts beaming,
The golden eagles also, that floated above the army
    Just like real eagles; –

The bronze-skinned Zouaves with ardent faces,
And their wild chants whose sound engulfed them,
– When three hundred cannons kept the beat for them,
    – In the furnace of Alma![23] –

And then, Sebastopol! – city of somber ravines,
Dark debris of an old world where there were giants,
The infernal iron collars crowning its hills,
    The cannons that strangled it, gaping!

VIII

Now, my verse grows faint. – O bitter satires!
Radiant Inkermann! Mournful and quiet songs,
Silence! – One must know how to forget on one's

---

[22]Lourmel: General Frédéric Henri Le Normand de Lourmel, who was killed at the Battle of Inkermann, 1854, during the Crimean War.

[23]Alma: The Battle of the Alma, 1854, in the Crimean War.

      knees. –
But, only, Englishmen, by your proud defiances,
Stop jeering at the dead who died for you. –

IX

O my God! – If our great causes
Predestined a noble child!...
. . . .
The throne hides things well
From the eyes of a shuddering dreamer. –
Height of human vanities,
At its feet bleed quite a few hatreds,
Often it covers its sorrow well!...
The somber crowds sit on the sill...
A fir tree covered in white ermine
Has a scepter and laurels for boughs...
It is made of four planks,
      Absolutely just like a coffin! –

Other Books by the Publisher

Fanchette's Pretty Little Foot by Restif de La Bretonne

Je M'Accuse... by Léon Bloy

My Hospitals & My Prisons by Paul Verlaine

Salvation Through the Jews by Léon Bloy

Words of a Demolitions Contractor by Léon Bloy

Cellulely by Paul Verlaine

Ecclesiastical Laurels by Jacques Rochette de la Morlière

Flowers of Bitumen by Émile Goudeau

Songs for Her & Odes in Her Honor by Paul Verlaine

On Huysmans' Tomb by Léon Bloy

Ten Years a Bohemian by Émile Goudeau

The Soul of Napoleon by Léon Bloy

Blood of the Poor by Léon Bloy

Joan of Arc and Germany by Léon Bloy

A Platonic Love by Paul Alexis

The Revealer of the Globe: Christopher Columbus & His Future Beatification (Part One) by Léon Bloy

An Immodest Proposal by Dr. Helmut Schleppend

The Pornographer by Restif de La Bretonne

Style (Theory and History) by Ernest Hello

On the Threshold of the Apocalypse: 1913-1915 by Léon Bloy

She Who Weeps (Our Lady of La Salette) by Léon Bloy

The Sylph by Claude Prosper Jolyot de Crébillon (*fils*)

Voyage in France by a Frenchman by Paul Verlaine

Ourigan, Oregon by William Clark, Richard Robinson, and anonymous

Drowning by Yu Dafu

Cull of April by Francis Vielé-Griffin

The Misfortune of Monsieur Fraque by Paul Alexis

Fêtes Galantes & Songs Without Words by Paul Verlaine

Joys by Francis Vielé-Griffin

The Son of Louis XVI by Léon Bloy

Septentrion by Jean Raspail

The Resurrection of Villiers de l'Isle-Adam by Léon Bloy

Poems Saturnian by Paul Verlaine

The Biography of Léon Bloy: Memories of a Friend by René Martineau

Fredegund, France: A Book of Poetry by Richard Robinson

The Good Song by Paul Verlaine

Swans by Francis Vielé-Griffin

Constantinople and Byzantium by Léon Bloy

Enamels and Cameos by Théophile Gautier

Four Years of Captivity in Cochons-sur-Marne: 1900-1904 by Léon Bloy

Dark Minerva: Prolegomena: The Moral Construction of Dante's Divine Comedy by Giovanni Pascoli

What is Fascism: Discourses and Polemics by Giovanni Gentile

The Desperate Man by Léon Bloy

Meditations of a Solitary in 1916 by Léon Bloy

The Ride of Yeldis & Other Poems by Francis Vielé-Griffin

Silvie & The Chimeras by Gérard de Nerval

Italian Nationalism by Enrico Corradini

A Silver-Grey Death and *Drowning* by Yu Dafu

Doctrines of Hatred, Part I: Anti-Semitism by Anatole Leroy-Beaulieu

Rhymes of Joy by Théodore Hannon

Windows and Doors by Richard Robinson

The Perverted Peasant or *The Dangers of the City* (Parts 1 and 2) by Restif de la Bretonne